Mirroring One Another, Reflecting the Divine:

The Franciscan-Muslim Journey into God

Volume 13   2009

Spirit and Life: Essays on Contemporary Franciscanism serves as a vehicle for the publication of papers presented at various conferences, symposia, and/or workshops that seek to bring the Franciscan tradition into creative dialogue with contemporary theology, philosophy, and history. The journal is an occasional publication.

During the fiftieth anniversary year of The Franciscan Institute (1991), the publication of this journal was a re-founding of an earlier Franciscan Institute Series entitled *Spirit and Life*, established in 1948 by the Reverend Philotheus Boehner, O.F.M., one of the co-founders and first director of The Franciscan Institute.

Copyright © 2009
Franciscan Institute Publications
Saint Bonaventure University
Saint Bonaventure, NY 14778

ISBN: 1-57659-157-3

Library of Congress Control Number:
2009930336

Printed in the United States of America
by BookMasters, Inc.
Ashland, Ohio

Spirit and Life

Essays on Contemporary Franciscanism

Volume 13   *2009*

Mirroring One Another, Reflecting the Divine: The Franciscan-Muslim Journey into God

Series Editor:
Michael F. Cusato, O.F.M.

Volume Editor:
Daria Mitchell, O.S.F.

CONTENTS

Preface v

Jan Hoeberichts
    Francis's View of Islam in the Mirror of God 1

F. Betul Cavdar
    *Mirroring God: Metaphors of the Mirror
    in the Writings of Ibn Arabi and St. Clare of Assisi* 39

Michael D. Calabria, O.F.M.
    Ibn al-Fāriḍ: Francis's Sufi Contemporary 53

Paul Lachance, O.F.M.
    Angela of Foligno: Poverty/Fana 75

Robert Lentz, O.F.M.
    Of Veils and Mirrors 103

PREFACE

On June 7-10, 2007 the Franciscan Institute sponsored the Seventh National Franciscan Forum on the theme: *Daring to Embrace the Other: Franciscans and Muslims in Dialogue* at the Franciscan Retreat Center in Colorado Springs, Colorado. This was an important, if not historic event in the life of the Franciscan Family in North America, especially given the context in which the gathering was held: almost six years after the events of September 11, 2001 and four years after the American invasion of the country of Iraq. As a result of these terrible and tragic events, relations between members of the two religious communities of Islam and Christianity have become increasingly more tense, even acrimonious. Hence, the felt-need on the part of many to attempt to address, from the perspective of the Franciscan tradition, questions prompted by mutual suspicion, stereotypes and open hostility in order to open up the possibility, even in small ways, of building bridges of understanding and respect between the faithful of these two religious traditions. To that end, the Seventh National Forum offered its participants four scholarly papers and two contemporary reflections on how one might approach this particular form of inter-religious dialogue in our own time. The symposium also included an opening call to prayer, cross-cultural liturgies and a visit to a local Muslim center. The reconciling purpose of the event was visualized in a powerfully affecting icon by the noted iconographer, Robert Lentz, O.F.M., of the embrace of Francis and Malek al-Kamil in the tent of the Sultan. The results were published in volume 12 of the *Spirit & Life Series*.[1]

The Seventh National Forum provided participants with a solid historical grounding for the possibilities of dialogue. The participants,

---

[1] *Daring to Embace the Other: Franciscans and Muslims in Dialogue*, Spirit and Life 12 (St. Bonaventure, NY: Franciscan Institute Publications, 2008).

however, voiced their desire to explore a bit further the rich spiritual traditions binding (and sometimes demarcating) these two historic religions and to delve more deeply into contemporary strategies of dialogue. Hence: the calling of the Eighth National Forum the following year, on June 16-19, 2008, again in Colorado Springs. It is the Eighth National Franciscan Forum that is the subject of this present volume of papers.

The theme chosen for the Eighth Forum flows from its predecessor, but takes a new and more interior direction with the theme: *Mirroring One Another, Reflecting the Divine: The Franciscan-Muslim Journey into God*. The title of the symposium was meant to call to mind both the journey motif so beloved of Bonaventure of Bagnoregio (in his *Itinerarium mentis in Deum*) as well as the image of the mirror used to such striking effect by Clare of Assisi in her own writings. We who share a common spiritual journey of faith and stand before the mirror, see within the Mirror (which is God) not only ourselves but also each other, as reflections of the Divine whom we seek and who seeks us. To actualize this reflective image, the symposium was structured in pairs so that the presentations of Christians and Muslims mirrored each other, as it were, by inviting a member of the other faith, as much as possible, to comment on the perspectives just shared by the presenter.

To explore this perspective, the Franciscan Institute invited from Holland one of the persons within the larger Franciscan Family who has been most responsible for reviving our knowledge of Francis's vision of the non-Christian Other in the last two decades: Jan Hoeberichts, whose two English-language volumes have been instrumental in opening up the vision of Francis to countless readers.[2] His presentation – "Francis's View of Islam in the Mirror of God" – takes as its point of departure Francis's unusual formulations in his *Salutation of the Virtues* which give us a key to a different manner of approaching one who is on a similar path of the discovery of God.

After mirroring the opening lecture by Hoeberichts, Dr. Fatima Betul Cavdar then delivered a presentation on two contemporaries of Francis of Assisi, one Muslim and the other Christian: "Mirroring God: Metaphors of Mirror in the Writings of Ibn 'Arabi and St. Clare

---

[2] J. Hoeberichts, *Francis and Islam* (Quincy, IL: Franciscan Press, 1997); and idem, *Paradise Restored: The Social Ethics of Francis of Assisi* (Quincy, IL: Franciscan Press, 2004).

of Assisi." Her talk was commented on by Michael Blastic, O.F.M., a renowned expert on the writings of Clare. Robert Lentz, O.F.M., created a striking iconographical image to underscore the central theme of the conference, employing an actual mirror in which participants, both Muslim and Christian, could see themselves reflected.

The following day, Michael Calabria, O.F.M. – also a presenter at the Seventh Forum – explored another contemporary of Francis: "Ibn al-Farid: Francis's Sufi Contemporary," showing some striking similarities between the two men of faith. A similar trajectory was followed by Paul Lachance, O.F.M., this time from the Christian perspective: "Angela da Foligno: Poverty/*fana*," illustrating the close association between the mystical understanding of poverty and its Islamic correlative in the concept of *fana*.

The conference concluded with presentations by two men who have been actively engaged in the inter-faith dialogue today: Imam Yahya Hendi and Adam Bunnell, O.F.M. Conv. Indeed, until recently, both had worked together at a center for inter-religious understanding at Georgetown University. These more free wheeling, contemporary reflections, filled with lively anecdotes about the joys and difficulties of engaging on this common journey, are not included here in published form.

It is the hope and prayer of the presenters at both the Seventh and Eighth National Franciscan Forums that these volumes of collected papers will serve as an inspiration to readers to set their feet upon this most urgent and holy journey of encounter and thereby discover the One who is wholly beyond yet wholly within.

Michael F. Cusato, O.F.M.
Director, Franciscan Institute
15 May 2009

Francis's View of Islam in the Mirror of God

Jan Hoeberichts

Theology is historical

As the title "Francis's View of Islam in the Mirror of God" indicates, this address will be theological rather than historical. But then, any theology, any God-talk is always and essentially historical so that I have to take the historical aspect into account as well. For theological reflection does not take place in a vacuum, but is always the reflection of a historical person, essentially conditioned and limited by the historical context, by the time and place where he or she lives, its culture, its ideas, its values, and so on. The scholastics expressed this insight, fundamental to any theological research, in the famous adage: *Nihil in intellectu nisi prius fuerit in sensu*, (there is nothing in our intellect, in our mind that has not previously passed by our senses).[1] All that we know, therefore, is the fruit of what we see, hear, touch, feel, experience and our reflection on these experiences which again takes place within the context of the language we have learned, the ideas we have come across, the experiences we have gained. Even in his or her highest mystical experiences, a person remains always this socially, culturally and morally conditioned and limited human being.[2]

---

[1] *Summa Theologica* I, q. 84, art. 7. Thomas Aquinas steers a middle course between *empiricism*, only what can be verified by science exists, and *spiritualism*, the true reality is to be found in the world of ideas; all that we see is but an illusion. Another relevant scholastic philosophical principle states: *cognitum est in cognoscente secundum modum cognoscentis*, "Whatever is known, exists in the knower according to the mode of the knower," S Th I, q. 7, art 4, or more generally: *Quidquid recipitur ad modum recipientis recipitur*, "Whatever is received, is received according to the mode of the receiver." It is therefore important to know who the knower or the receiver is! These principles have their origin in Greek Aristotelian philosophy which reached Europe via Avicenna, *Ibn Sina*, born in Afshjanah near Bukhara (Uzbekistan) in 980 and died in Hamadan (North Iran) in 1037, and Averroes, *Ibn Rushd*, born in Cordoba (Spain) in 1126 and died in Marrakech (Morocco) in 1198.

[2] Bernard of Clairvaux (1090-1153), one of the great Catholic mystics, was a fervent crusade preacher. He pitched his preaching of the second crusade (1146-1148)

This fundamental law of our human historical existence, even God, so to say, cannot circumvent. God's revelation to Jesus took place in the language of the Torah and the Prophets, as heard and reflected upon within the context of the Palestine of his days, a country occupied and exploited by the Romans. Otherwise Jesus would simply not have been able to understand God's word, God's revelation. Similarly the prophet Mohammad received his revelations in Arabic and not, for example, Chinese, and within the socio-economic, cultural and religious context of the Arabia of his days.

CREATIVITY, NOT REPETITION

These limitations imply, as a necessary and unavoidable consequence, that we, whoever we are, whether pope, bishop, theologian or "ordinary faithful," cannot satisfy ourselves with just literally repeating biblical or koranic texts, spoken and written down many centuries ago in an entirely different world, as if therewith we would be able to solve the problems of our present, modern society. Rather we have always to ask about the circumstances of time and place in which the historical Jesus or the historical Mohammad made a certain pronouncement to find out what they really meant and to creatively rethink this and transpose it to our present time in order thus not only to safeguard the letter, but – and this is far more important – the spirit! Creativity and not repetition is what we need today, well aware of the historical condition of all, even religious statements. And it would not be a superfluous luxury if especially all those who claim authority in religious matters would regularly repeat the above adage for the benefit of themselves and of those whom they have to help to grow (authority, it is all too often forgotten, is derived from the Latin *augere*, to grow, to increase, to strengthen). Such a repetition might, paradoxically, help them to

---

around the theme of the crusade as the beginning of the time of salvation, with reference to 2 Cor 6:2: *Ecce nunc tempus acceptabile, ecce nunc dies salutis*. He also called the second crusade an *artificium*, a piece of art. He even defended the thesis that "to inflict death or to die for Christ is no sin, but rather an abundant claim to glory. In the first case one gains for Christ, and in the second one gains Christ himself ... If a knight of Christ kills an evildoer, he is not the killer of a human being but, if I may so put it, a killer of evil." Further, see Jan Hoeberichts, *Francis and Islam* (Quincy, Il: Franciscan Press, 1997), 15-16; 204-05.

Francis's View of Islam in the Mirror of God

avoid the repetitions which they all too often limit themselves to, as is, for example, the case in recent Roman statements on church, mission, evangelization and interreligious dialogue.[3] These repetitions of what in the past was defined as doctrine of the church, often only lead to the condemnation and ostracization of men and women who to the best of their ability try to keep God's word alive and to find a creative answer to the problems of our days.[4]

FRANCIS, READING THE SIGNS OF THE TIME

Although Francis was not a professional theologian, or maybe precisely because he was not and had rather committed himself to live "simply and without gloss" (Test 39)[5] according to the model of Jesus' gospel in the place where God had brought him,[6] Francis felt free to creatively approach even papal and conciliar statements, to question them and to propose very unique and original solutions to the vital problems of his time. For his gospel freedom enabled and empowered

---

[3] See, for example, the declaration *Dominus Jesus* (August 6, 2000) of the Congregation for the Doctrine of the Faith, and its subsequent doctrinal notes on church and ecumenism: *Ad catholicam* (June 29, 2007) and on evangelization and interreligious dialogue: *Doctrinal note on some aspects of evangelization* (December 3, 2007). It is remarkable indeed to see the frequent use of verbs like "to recall, to reiterate, to set forth again" in the declaration *Dominus Jesus*. In fact, this declaration describes its purpose as "to set forth again the doctrine of the Catholic faith ... refuting specific positions that are erroneous or ambiguous. For this reason, the Declaration takes up what has been taught in previous magisterial documents, in order to reiterate certain truths that are part of the Church's faith" (3).

[4] Theologians who have recently been scrutinized, especially on matters of Christology and of religious pluralism, are Jacques Dupuis (1998), Roger Haight (2000); Jon Sobrino (2007); Peter C. Phan (2007).

[5] "The Latin word *glossa* was a technical term for the learned annotations which were made to the Scriptures and other legal texts. And the expression *sine glossa* resounded like a slogan throughout the thirteenth century. It symbolized the resistance against an overly subtle explanation of the Bible which caused the Bible's own strength to be lost in finespun arguments that extinguished the spirit, and against an interpretation of the rules so learned that nothing was left of them or that they were even turned into their opposites." Gerard Pieter Freeman and Hans Sevenhoven, "The Legacy of a Poor Man. Commentary on the Testament of Francis of Assisi," Part 5, in *FrancDigest* 6, 1 (April 1996): 1-26, here 13.

[6] For me Francis is a living illustration of the axiom of liberation theology that commitment is the first act of theology!

him to look with new eyes at the world around him or, to use the expression of Vatican II, to read afresh the signs of the time in the light of the gospel, not burdened by all the learned glosses that often took the edge off Jesus' challenging words and example. Thus Francis obtained an understanding of God and God's will that remained closed to many of his contemporaries, especially those in authority, who, because of their powerful "God-given" position, were often deeply involved in and committed to maintaining their world in the name of God – an attitude that they justified by their interpretation of God's word, – while, as we will see, Francis, guided by God's revelation, decided to leave that same world.

QUESTIONS TO BE ANSWERED

Who was the God whom Francis discovered in his historical context, at the time and place where he lived, and who led him to his controversial decision?[7] Or, to use the words of the title of this address, which God was reflected in the mirror in which Francis kept looking in order to unravel the difficult situations, often situations of life and death, that he was confronted with in the turbulent and violent days of his time? Which special aspects of the divine reality did he see, while they remained hidden to others? And what was that special place, that vantage point from which Francis looked at God and the world and which led him to draw such radically different conclusions from the ecclesiastical authorities of his time? These are the questions I will try to answer, well aware that I, too, am historically conditioned by my past and present, and especially by my stay of twenty-eight years in Pakistan, where I witnessed the enormous problems a developing Asian Muslim nation was confronted with and where, together with my Franciscan sisters and brothers, I had to try and answer the question of our Franciscan identity in such a country: a search that led me, under the guidance and inspiration of Asian liberation theolo-

---

[7] Not only did Francis's father strongly object to his decision to leave the world and start a new way of life (1C 12-15), also the bishop of Assisi (AP 17) and the pope and cardinals of the Roman curia advised against it (AP 33-34).

gians[8] and Franciscan scholars like David Flood,[9] to develop a more contextual and liberation theological reading of Francis's writings, and especially also of Francis's view of Muslims and their religion. In this light a better title for my address would have been: My view on the way Francis looked at Islam in the mirror of God. A more modest title, indeed, which, however, does not lessen my personal conviction that this approach reveals many important and valuable elements that also today can contribute to a positive and more creative approach to the relationship between Islam and Christianity than the envisaged interreligious dialogue between Muslim scholars and Roman authorities which, on the face of it, is no more than a polite exchange of the often repeated similarities and differences between the two religions without touching the fundamental question of the historically conditioned character of all revelation, including both Muslim and Christian.

THE MIRROR OF GOD

In order to know the mirror of God that Francis held before himself and now holds before us, we need not make lengthy studies about God in the writings of Francis or his early biographies, though they are definitely very helpful.[10] For towards the end of his life Francis wrote in his own hand his *Praises of God* in which he poetically sums up his profound personal understanding of God as it had developed after his conversion and found its culmination in the mystical experience on La Verna. This hymn with its many names of God has in the view of several authors been inspired by the recitation of the ninety-nine most

---

[8] To mention just a few theologians whom I met at the First Asian Theological Conference of the Ecumenical Association of Third World Theologians (EATWOT) which was held in Wennappuwa, Sri Lanka, in January 1979: Samuel Ryan, Aloys Pieris, Sebastian Kappen, Tissa Balasuriya. See my "Towards an Asian Theology," in *Al-Mushir* 22, 2 (Summer 1980): 74-89.

[9] David Flood, *Die Regula non bullata der Minderbrüder* (Werl: Dietrich-Coelde-Verlag, 1967); *Francis of Assisi and the Franciscan Movement* (Quezon City: FIA Contact Publications, 1989); *Work for Everyone Francis of Assisi and the Ethic of Service* (Quezon City: CCFMC Office for Asia/Oceania, 1997). Those familiar with Flood's interpretation of early Franciscan history will recognize many of his ideas in my text.

[10] See, for example, the collection of articles published on the occasion of the eighth centenary of Francis's birth (1182-1982) under the title: *L'Esperienza di Dio in Francesco d'Assisi* (Rome, 1982).

beautiful names of Allah,[11] which Francis had witnessed among the Muslims and which had deeply impressed him.[12] The same inspiration is very evident also from the original, unique expression Francis coined after his return to Italy in some of his letters and in his *Testament* where he speaks about "the written most holy names and words of the Lord" (LtCl 1,3,12; 1LtCus 2; Test 12), a combination that is nowhere else found among his contemporaries.[13]

PRAISES OF GOD

Just as any other text, so also Francis's *Praises of God* can be approached in a variety of ways. We can ask when and for whom it was written, as Michael Cusato did at last year's forum where he argued that the *Praises of God* are not only Francis's own personalized version of the ninety-nine most beautiful names of Allah, but that Francis prayed in this Islamic manner precisely because he was very much preoccupied by the fate of the sultan as the sultan's life was being threatened by the unholy conspiracy between pope Honorius III and the Holy Roman Emperor Frederick II who in 1223 agreed to launch a new crusade.[14]

---

[11] The list of the ninety-nine most beautiful names of Allah can easily be found on the internet in various languages.

[12] See Kathleen A. Warren, *Daring to Cross the Threshold: Francis of Assisi encounters Sultan Malek al-Kamil* (Rochester, MN: Sisters of St. Francis, 2003), Appendix I, 122-28.

[13] See my *Francis and Islam*, 89-90, 244, note 102. I notice that authors try in different ways to explain Francis's interest in God's names by referring to the writings of Denis the Pseudo-Areopagite (Cornet); the high-priestly prayer in the gospel of John (Asseldonk, Viviani) and/or Francis's daily prayer of the psalms and the Our Father (Lehmann). They fail, however, to explain the unique combination of "names and words" which is only found in Francis's writings, when he urges people to have a great reverence both for the most holy Body and Blood of the Lord, and for his most holy written names and words. The combination "names and words" is missing in Francis's *Letter to the Order* 34-37, where he, in a Eucharistic context, speaks only about the "holy words." I think that there are good arguments to attribute this omission of "names" to the activities of a secretary. See the commentary on these verses in my "Francis' Letter to all the Brothers (Letter to the Entire Order): Title, Theme, Structure and Language," in *Collectanea Franciscana* 78 (2008): 5-85, here 49-51.

[14] Michael F. Cusato, "From Damietta to La Verna. The Impact on Francis of his Experience in Egypt," in *Daring to Embrace the Other: Franciscans and Muslims in Dialogue*, Spirit and Life 12 (St. Bonaventure, NY: Franciscan Institute Publications, 2008), 81-112.

However, in this year's address I want to look more at the content, at the theology, the God-talk, it contains. In the context of this forum, a first question that comes to mind is: how far are the names of God in Francis's *Praises* also found in the list of Allah's names and in formulas used in Muslim prayer? There are indeed some remarkable similarities. For example, Francis opens his *Praises* with: "You are the holy Lord, the only God; You are the most high, you are the all-powerful King' and closes them with: You are ... the all-powerful God, the merciful Savior." In the words: "You are the only God," we hear in fact an echo of the Muslim confession of faith, the *shadaha*: "There is no god, but God." Further we meet here the first four names of the list of Allah's names: *Ar-Rahman, Ar-Rahim* (the Merciful), *Al-Malik* (the King), *Al-Quddus* (the Most Holy). A further study might come up with other interesting results, but here I want to limit myself to just two observations.

God, the Merciful

First, Francis ends with naming God "merciful." This is the most used title for God in Islam which expresses this essential quality of Allah in a double name: *Ar-Rahman, Ar-Rahim*. As part of the formula *Bismillah ar-Rahman, ar-Rahim*, the invocation of the Merciful opens all *Suras* of the Koran, except the ninth. Further, it is used in the Muslim daily prayer and on many other occasions both in private and in public life.[15] Francis uses this name only once more, namely in his prayer at the end of his *Letter to the Entire Order* or rather the *Letter to all his Brothers* (50), a letter in which, remarkably, several other expressions occur that show the influence of Francis's stay among the Muslims. One of them is the name: the All-powerful, which is the object of my second observation.[16]

---

[15] Besides at the beginning of the *Suras*, except *Sura* 9, *Ar-Rahman* occurs fifty-seven times in the Koran and *Ar-Rahim* 117 times.

[16] Other possible indications of Muslim influence are found in LtOrd 4: "When you hear his name, the name of the Son of the Most high [in the call to prayer] ... adore his name with fear and reverence, prostrate on the ground"; and the repeated emphasis on "pleasing God": LtOrd 15, 42, 50. See my "Francis' Letter to all the Brothers," 15, 27-28, 77.

God, the All-powerful

This name occurs twice, at the beginning and at the end of Francis's Praises, and appears to have become his favorite name of God after his return from the sultan. He uses it in chapter 16 of the *Earlier Rule* when he writes about what the brothers should preach to the Saracens "when they see that it pleases God" (7); in the *Letter to the Rulers* 7 and *First Letter to the Custodians* 8 where he writes about the daily call to prayer, and especially in the *Letter to all the Brothers* where the name of God, the All-powerful, occurs no less than five times, notably in v. 9 where Francis in a personal improvisation on a text of the Book of Tobit defines the mission of his brothers in the world as to "bear witness to God's voice in word and deed and bring everyone to know that there is no one who is all-powerful except Him," – a formula which definitely carries Muslim overtones.[17] But rather than continuing along this road, I shall in what follows, in line with the title of this address, concentrate on studying the Praises of God as a mirror. Looking in this mirror, which name or names of God stand out and have exercised a real impact on Francis's view of Islam and its faithful followers? In my opinion there are two names in particular that deserve our attention. The first name: God is humility, is, according to the best of my knowledge, not present among the ninety-nine beautiful names of Allah, and may precisely for this reason throw more light on a truly Franciscan approach to Islam and to interreligious dialogue in general, while the second: God is patience, is identical with the ninety-ninth – the last, but certainly not the least – of the most beautiful names of Allah: *As-Shabur*, the Patient, the Timeless One.

You are humility

Humility is certainly not a virtue in favor among Christians today, let alone of other people. People question even whether humility is really a virtue. For in our present society everything appears to center around riches and power as means towards the self-assertion of the individual. Moreover, when humility is praised, it is often done by the rich and powerful. They like to recommend humility to the poor,

---

[17] The other four times are in LtOrd 13, 48, 50, 52. It is a pity that the new English translation [FA:ED] uses "all-powerful" and "almighty" interchangeably.

humbled and maginalized people as the virtue which will guarantee them a high place in heaven. They abuse humility in their desire to safeguard their own position and to keep the poor masses down in the place where they belong and cannot form a threat to them and to their style of life which they claim as their God-given right! But whereas the virtue and the practice of humility pose a real problem for many of Jesus' followers today,[18] Francis becomes lyrical when he touches the subject of humility. Thus he writes in his First Admonition:

> See, each day [the Son of God] humbles himself as when he came from the royal throne into the Virgin's womb; each day he himself comes to us appearing in humble form; each day he comes down from the bosom of the Father upon the altar in the hands of a priest (Adm 1:16-18).

Or as he writes in the *Letter to the Order*:

> O wonderful loftiness and stupendous humanity![19] O sublime humility! O humble sublimity, that the Lord of the universe, God and Son of God, so humbles himself that for our salvation he hides himself under an ordinary piece of bread! (LtOrd 27-28).[20]

See, brothers, the humility of our God

However, the lyrical Francis does not start floating above the clouds. He is personally well aware that his brothers, and especially his brother priests, have great difficulty with this virtue. After his lyrical outburst Francis continues with a very down-to-earth admonition:

---

[18] See, for example, the articles in *Franciscaans Leven* 90, 1 (February 2007) devoted to humility.

[19] The Latin text has here *dignatio*. The new English translation translates this by "dignity" (*dignitas*; FAED 1, 118). The noun *dignatio*, however, refers rather to the fact that God deigned to become one of us, humans, in Jesus' incarnation. I prefer therefore the translation "humanity," the *humanitas* that is spoken of in the Letter to Titus 3:4. If this translation is considered too free, an alternative would be "condescension."

[20] About this hymn, its relation with the early Christian hymn in Philippians 2:6-11, and the implications of the admonition to the brothers to humble themselves, see my "The Letter to all the Brothers," 34-39.

"See, brothers, the humility of our God ... and humble yourselves" – a down-to-earth admonition, indeed, for, etymologically, the Latin word *humilis* is derived from *humus*, soil, earth, from which God fashioned the first human.[21] Following this track, we might discover beautiful insights into the meaning and importance of humility, but it might also lead us away from the way Francis, in his historical context, had come to see the humility of God. For, it is only from this context and not through etymological similarities that we have to interpret Francis's fascination with humility,[22] and especially with humility as a name of God. It was the outcome of a long learning process marked by many events but, as he himself wrote in his *Testament* (1-3), started in all earnest with his stay among the lepers.[23]

---

[21] Cf. Gen 2:7, though the Latin text uses here the word *limus*.

[22] For a more extensive study of Francis's understanding of humility as a virtue, see my *Paradise Restored The Social Ethics of Francis of Assisi, A Commentary on Francis'* Salutation of the Virtues (Quincy, Il: Franciscan Press, 2004), 93-108, 206-14.

[23] In contrast with several later biographers who emphasize the encounter with one leper (L3C 11; 2C 9; LMj 1:5), Francis in his *Testament*, looking back at the beginning, considers his stay among the lepers the turning point in his life. Thus Francis appears to indicate that his conversion did not happen in a single moment of divine enlightenment, as the biographers seem to suggest, but rather was the outcome of a hard learning process which, as he recalls, slowly "turned what had seemed bitter to [him] into sweetness" (3). See my "The Justification of a Choice" in *Franciscan Digest* 12, 2 (September 2002): 10-23.

As regards Celano's and Bonaventure's hint that, in line with Matt 25: 40, Francis met Christ in the leper who mysteriously disappeared, it may be noticed that Francis never quotes this text of Matthew. I hesitate, therefore, to give such a profoundly religious interpretation to Francis's stay among the lepers, especially since he was still very much searching for his direction in life, as the story about the discovery of the foundational gospel texts in the church of St. Nicholas clearly indicates (AP 10-11). Thus I would agree with Cusato who writes that "Francis encountered, perhaps for the first time in his life, truly suffering human beings: men and women ... whom the Assisi of his youth had taught him were of no account, people to be avoided, shunned and despised.... The lepers were no empty ciphers, no mere vehicles, through whom Francis encountered what really mattered: Christ" (Michael F. Cusato, "To do penance / Facere poenitentiam," in *The Cord* 57 (2007): 1-24, here 10-11). For the preference to be given to the story in AP 10-11 above the story in 1Cel 22, where Francis alone hears these foundational gospel texts during Mass at the Portiuncula chapel, see A. Jansen, "Franciscus ontdekt het evangelie," in *Franciscaans Leven* 66 (1983): 2-12.

Francis's change of place

This fascination with the humility of God was certainly not something Francis had received from home. He had certainly heard about the poor and humble Jesus, particularly during the Christmas season. But it is doubtful whether these stories had really touched him. He appears to be far more under the spell of his dreams about power and prestige, trying to become a noble man (1C 4-5; 2C 6).[24] His fascination with humility started slowly growing only when the Lord himself – who else? – led him among the lepers and thus introduced him to an entirely different place than he was used to as the son of the rich merchant Pietro Bernardone (Test 1-3). Thanks to this radical change of place – he was really uprooted! – Francis's eyes were opened to a reality that was unknown to him before. In this new place among the lepers – *inter leprosos*, the preposition *inter* is very important and returns in *Earlier Rule* 16, where Francis speaks about brothers wanting to go among the Saracens, *inter Saracenos* – Francis was able to see with his own eyes and to experience in his own person what riches and power did to people. He saw how people were thrown out of society and, in a kind of burial rite, so to say, buried alive in a leper house. Confronted with this inhuman reality, Francis went through, what Schillebeeckx called, a contrast experience.[25] Francis felt vividly and almost instinctively that what was happening in the leper house, shouldn't be; that it was totally against God's intentions with humankind. Did God not say that we have to love our neighbor as ourselves? This inhuman sin-

---

[24] According to Manselli and others, Francis joined Count Gentile (L3C 5) to fight in a papal war, a crusade, against the emperor's forces in Apulia (Raoul Manselli, *St. Francis of Assisi* [Chicago: Franciscan Herald Press, 1988], 47-48). Helene Nolthenius rejects this view, because Assisi was an imperial stronghold which gave a hearty welcome to the excommunicated Bishop Lupold of Worms, delegate of emperor Philip of Swabia. At that time Assisi was thinking of acknowledging the emperor's rights in Central Italy in exchange for his support against Perugia. It is very unlikely that in these circumstances a young man of Assisi was ready to join the papal troops. Helene Nolthenius, *Een man uit het dal van Spoleto. Franciscus tussen zijn tijdgenoten* (Amsterdam: Em. Querido, 1988), 53-56; 323.

[25] Edward Schillebeeckx, "De kerk als sacrament van dialoog," in *Tijdschrift voor Theologie* 8 (1968): 155-69, here 166-67; id., "Theologische draagwijdte van het magisteriële spreken over sociaal-politieke kwesties," *Conciklium* 4, 6 (juni 1968): 21-40, here 30-34. Also: Leonhard Lehmann, "Franziskus und die utopische Bewegung heute," in *Franziskanische Studien* 67 (1985): 86-113, here 90.

ful situation had to end. And Francis set himself to do so by, as he writes in his *Testament*, showing them mercy: *misericordia*, that is, in a merciless and heartless world, he showed his heart, his *cor* to these miserable people, *miseri*.[26] Thus he did what lay within his possibilities to counteract this degrading situation in which people, contrary to God's intentions, were sacrificed to the intentions of Assisi's citizens to increase their riches and power and to cast away those who could not contribute to the achievement of those goals.

"I left the world"

And, after a little while – it all took time and nothing happened in a flash as in the case of St. Paul's conversion – Francis decided – it was in the year 1206 – "to leave the world" (Test 3). We have to understand this very concretely and not in some vague, general sense, as if Francis wanted to join a religious community. No, as the outcome of the learning process among the lepers, Francis decided to leave the world of Assisi and all it stood for: its entire social, economic, cultural and ethical system. He did not want to be a part of a world that because of its socio-economic goals was ready to dehumanize people and to condemn them to a life of poverty, misery and destitution, preferably outside the walls of the city. He did not want to belong to a world that sacrificed people on the altar of mammon to safeguard their own interests and to promote their own glory and power. It is this hard, heartless and merciless world that Francis rejected, at the same time initiating his search, first alone, and later, from 1208 onward, together with his brothers, how to build, not just with words, but through deeds,[27] a society in accordance with God's intentions with humankind, or, as Francis says, a society where people "through their holy deeds give

---

[26] Remarkable here is the use of the Latin verb *facere*. When he was among the lepers, *facere paenitentiam* meant for Francis first and foremost *facere misericordiam*. To "do" mercy was for him in the given situation the first concrete implementation of "doing" penance.

[27] See, besides the first sentence of Francis's *Testament*: "The Lord gave me, brother Francis, thus to begin doing penance," the repeated emphasis on *opera* vs. *verba*: Adm 6:3; 9:4; ER 11:6; 17:3; LtOrd 8-9; and on *(sancta) operatio*: Adm 21:2; ER 7:12; 17:11; LR 10:8; 2 LtF 53; Test 39. In fact, Test 39: *et cum sancta operatione observetis usque in finem* is the very last admonition Francis gives to his brothers.

birth to Jesus" and thus continue Jesus' liberating, life-giving mission in the world (2LtF 53).[28]

The discovery of true humility

The experiences of injustice and division caused by the rich and the powerful to the detriment of the poor and the lepers form the historical context in which Francis and his brothers were able to develop, against the stream, a different understanding of humility. Gospel texts and stories that previously had not made a great impact, now came to life at their new place at the margin of society. True humility, they discovered, had nothing to do with the humility that the rich forced upon the poor, the lepers and the beggars along the wayside to keep them down in the place where they belong. To try and justify this humiliating and dehumanizing behavior by appealing to the humility to which all Christians are called, was just a hypocritical cover-up for something utterly evil: the marginalization and exclusion of people. True humility, the brothers now understood, is a virtue, that is, a *virtus*, or a God-given world-transforming power which in an exemplary form was present in the humble Jesus. He – they heard now loud and clear in many passages of Scripture – humbled himself by taking on a human form with no other aim in mind than through this act of humility, this sharing of our human earthly existence, to redeem us, humans, from the many ways in which we are held captive, and to restore paradise, the place God meant for us from the beginning (ER 23:1-3).[29]

---

[28] In doing so, the brothers clearly distance themselves from the world around them where, as Francis judges sharply, people "are still crucifying [Jesus] by delighting in vices and sins" (Adm 5:3) and thus continue to confirm the power of sin in the world with all its degrading and dehumanizing consequences. For Francis's deep awareness of the dehumanizing consequences of sin, see the text from Ps 22:4 which Francis quotes in OfP 4:7 and 2LtF 46: "I am a worm and not a man; the scorn of men and the outcast of the people." See my "'De Heer heerst vanaf het kruishout.' Enkele gedachten bij Psalm 7 van Franciscus' Officie van de Mysteries van de Heer," in *Franciscaans Leven* 87 (2004): 111-22, note 12.

[29] In ER 23:1-3 Francis gives a brief summary of salvation history which he describes, not as something of the past but, speaking in the first person plural, as something that we are now involved in. In v. 1 he speaks about creation, which ends with "giving thanks to God ... who made us in God's own image and likeness and placed us in paradise." Paradise is the place which God destined for us, humans, and where we belong. But then the anticlimax comes, formulated in just one short sentence: "Through our own fault we fell" (2) and lost paradise! Yet, however tragic this fall is,

Humility as an act of solidarity

God's humility, as revealed in Jesus' incarnation, is thus first and foremost a freely chosen act of solidarity on the part of Jesus who, as he himself said, "did not come to be served but to serve" (Matt 20:28; ER 4:6) and instructed his followers that "whoever wants to be the greatest among you must be your servant" (Matt 20:27; ER 5:11). A freely chosen act of solidarity, thus, through which Jesus places himself at the service of humankind and, by preference, at the service of all people in material and spiritual need: not only the lame, the blind, the lepers but also the sinner and those in distress. It is this liberating humility of Jesus which Francis and his brothers want to follow in order to put an end to the inhuman conditions with which they are confronted in their historical context and to build a more human sister- and brotherhood, not on the basis of riches and power which divide, but on the basis of humility, of solidarity through service which brings people together in peace. One of the distinctive marks of such a society will be a true spirit of hospitality which welcomes "friend or foe, thief or robber" (ER 7:14), to sit around "the table of the Lord" (Test 22), as an evangelical alternative for the often hard, inhospitable and merciless mentality prevailing in the society of their day.

A first elaboration

Francis and his brothers elaborate this gradually won insight in various ways, the oldest one of which we find most probably in Earlier Rule 7.[30] In this chapter Francis and his brothers reflect on the work they are to do and how they are to do it if they want to work ac-

---

it is not the end. On the contrary, God continues the story with humankind. God who created us out of love, wills through that same love "to redeem us captives through [Jesus'] cross and blood and death" (3). By freeing us from our captivity, God opens for us the way to rise up again and restore paradise through our holy deeds, that is, through the practice of the God-given virtues (*virtutes*, powers) that overcome evil in all its many facets (SalV 9-14). See my *Paradise Restored*.

[30] The foundational guidelines of the beginning of Francis's movement are most probably found in chapters 1, 7 and 14. This view finds a confirmation in the description of the first beginnings of the brotherhood in Test 16-23, where Francis deals with the renunciation of all possessions (v. 13 = ch. 1), with work as service, being subject to all (vv. 19-20 = ch. 7) and with the peace mission of the brothers in the world (v. 23 = ch. 14).

cording to the model of the holy gospel that the Lord had revealed to them (Test 14). At the end of their reflections they determine that the brothers are not to accept leading positions of treasurers or overseers (*camerarii neque cancellarii*)[31] in the economy of Assisi or anywhere else. Rather, they are to be *minores*, lesser ones and *subditi*, subject to all in the houses where they serve (ER 7:1-2).[32] For the first time we meet here the word *subditus* which, with this typical Franciscan meaning, occurs another four times in Francis's writings, with or without reference to the 1Peter 2:13, where it is specifically mentioned that the followers of Jesus have to be "subject to every human creature *propter Deum*, because of God" (ER 16:6; 2 LtF 47). To be subject to every human creature appears thus to be a key concept of Francis's spirituality which, strangely enough, disappears from the official Rule of 1223, but makes its comeback in Francis's *Testament*, which underlines once more the importance Francis attaches to "being subject."

Another important element is the emphasis on work as service. For Francis and his brothers work is not a means to acquire and increase possessions and thereby to increase the divisions among people with all their damaging consequences like poverty and destitution, but also rivalry, competition, violence and war. Rather, work is a service which they render to society and for which they expect to receive in return whatever they need for their living and for exercising their responsibility, especially towards the needy lepers (ER 8:10). And so the brothers go through the world offering their services wherever they can, not appropriating anything for themselves, yet always ready to share the goods of God's creation with everyone and all. Thus they hope to counteract the evils of a world striving after ever greater wealth and possessions, and instead to promote unity, harmony and peace among the people. And if their peace efforts are not welcome and they

---

[31] Unfortunately, the new English translation translates the specific terms *camerarii* and *cancellarii* in a rather general way: "They may not be in charge" (*FAED* 1, 68). In his new critical edition of the *Earlier Rule*, Paolazzi reads: *camerarii neque cellarii*. See Carlo Paolazzi, "La Regola non Bullata dei Frati Minori (1221), dallo 'stemma codicum' al testo critico," in *AFH* 100 (2007): 5-148. The text of the Rule is on 125-48.

[32] By "houses" are meant farmhouses or leper houses, but also workshops that were attached to houses, for the brothers were allowed "to have the tools and instruments which they needed for their trades" (ER 7:9). The choice of Esser for *opportuna* instead of *necessaria* (see *FAED* 1, 69, note a) has been rejected on good grounds by Paolazzi in his new critical edition of the *Earlier Rule*. See previous note.

meet with hostility or even persecution, they will not retaliate. Rather, as chapter 14, just like chapter 7, one of the older and more original chapters of the *Earlier Rule*, states, they shall answer whatever evil is done to them by doing good – a fundamental rule of Franciscan gospel life which is repeated at the end of chapter 17 which forms the original conclusion of the *Earlier Rule*: "When we see or hear evil spoken or done or God blasphemed, let us speak well and do well (*bene dicamus et bene faciamus*) and praise God who is blessed forever" (ER 17:19).

Conflicting views

When Francis and his brothers were still in the early years of the development of their brotherhood, Innocent III decided in 1213 to start preparations for a new crusade in 1217.[33] From then on Francis and his brothers were exposed to an intense crusade propaganda: daily prayers, regular sermons and processions. All this made Francis and his brothers more than ever aware of the existence of the Saracens, the alleged enemies of Christians and Christianity. And while monasteries under the influence of this propaganda sold golden and silver chalices and other liturgical utensils to help finance the crusade,[34] Francis and his brothers decided quite the opposite: they would go among the Saracens and live there a life of humility in the spirit of the humble Jesus. For just as Francis, from his new place in society, was able to see the robbers in the forest not as his enemies but rather as victims of an unjust system that forced them to take what they needed to stay alive (AC 115), so he started also to look differently at those other enemies – the Saracens – and to question the war policies of the pope and the ambition of power behind them. Innocent wrote that he, as vicar of Christ the King, felt called by God to reconquer the Holy Land: the land that, as he formulated it rather dramatically, had been conquered by Christ's blood and hence was the inalienable property of the Christians. However, this way of thinking about war and power, even though theologically justified by the highest church authorities, was completely alien

---

[33] For a more detailed description of the well-planned and intense preparatory activities of Innocent III and their ideological background, see my *Francis and Islam*, 3-28.

[34] See James M. Powell, *Anatomy of a Crusade, 1213-1221* (Philadelphia: The University of Pennsylvania Press, 1986), 90-93.

to Francis.[35] And while the pope organized a crusade because of God, Francis went, as he writes himself, by divine inspiration to the Saracens not to fight against them (*contra*) but rather "to live among them (*inter*)" and, just as among the lepers, to enter a further learning process in this new place in an entirely new situation.

No arguments and disputes

It is quite evident that Francis felt himself driven by the insights in God's humility he had obtained by reflecting on his historical context in the light of Jesus and his gospel. This humility, this readiness to be subject, he did not see, however, in the activities of preachers like James of Vitry, the then bishop of Acre, in the Holy Land.[36] James took

---

[35] This view is rejected by a number of mainly non-Franciscan scholars. See, for example, Christoph T. Maier's, *Preaching the Crusades: Mendicant Friars and the Cross in the Thirteenth Century* (Cambridge: Cambridge University Press, 1994). He concludes his chapter on Francis and the fifth crusade without any examination of ER 16, saying: "[Francis's] overall objective was the same as that of the crusaders. Francis, like the crusaders, wanted to liberate the holy places in Palestine from Muslim rule. What was different was his strategy: Francis went beyond the idea of simply expelling the Muslims from where they interfered with Christian life. He wanted their total submission to the Christian faith. Short of this total submission there would be no peace; short of this, for Francis too, was the necessity, if not the duty, to crusade against the enemies of faith" (16-17). One wonders how this language about the "total submission" of the Muslims can be reconciled with Francis's admonition that the brothers' first way of living among the Saracens is "to be subject to every human creature because of God" (ER 16,6)? Even worse is the approach of John Tolan, *Le Saint chez le Sultan La rencontre de François d'Assise et de l'Islam. Huit siècles d'interprétation* (Paris: Seuil, 2007). In his very erudite and detailed history of the interpretation of Francis's visit with the sultan, Tolan does not even make a serious attempt to study in depth Francis's own interpretation of his visit to the sultan in ER 16 in its historical and literary context. In fact, quite unintelligibly, Tolan limits himself to a rather superficial and even incorrect and distorted two-page commentary on ER 16 (29-30), and dismisses offhand, without even mentioning their arguments, those who on the basis of a thorough analysis of ER 16 conclude that Francis's visit was essentially a mission of peace. In Tolan's view, these authors belong to those people who, living at the end of the twentieth and the dawn of the twenty-first century, denounce the crusades as pernicious, depraved manifestations of violence, rapacity and fanaticism and, out of the blue, start depicting Francis as a messenger of peace and opponent to the crusades, while no trace of Francis's hostility towards the crusades can be found in the sources. Their view on Francis's mission as a mission of peace must therefore, according to Tolan, be seen as a creation of the Franciscan historiography of the twentieth century that has no solid base in the documents (20-21; 465-66; 470; 474).

[36] On James of Vitry's ideas and policies, see my *Francis and Islam*, 32-41.

the words of Peter the Venerable, abbot of Cluny (1092-1156) very much to heart, that clerics, who were forbidden to carry arms, had nevertheless in a true crusader's spirit "to attack (*agredior*), not with arms, but with words."[37] And so James traveled around with a military escort, sitting on his high horse, to proclaim, as he writes it, the truth about Christ and to expose the lies of Mohammad. And when he could not preach directly to the Saracens because of the dangerous situation, he sent them letters with words of identical import. His whole approach bespeaks a feeling of superiority and not of humility. And all this in name of the truth which he possessed and which he had the duty to proclaim and, "welcome or unwelcome" (*opportune, inopportune*; 2 Tim 4:2) to insist on.

Francis rejected such strongly apologetic approaches. In his Rule he writes explicitly with reference to such preaching activities: the brothers who go "to live among the Saracens in the spirit of Jesus" (*spiritualiter conversari inter*)[38] are "not to engage in arguments or disputes" (ER 16:5-6). Does this mean that they have to obscure the truth in order not to hurt the others' feelings and keep peace and quiet? Francis certainly does not want to hurt people, but to approach them with kindness and respect, and to create a courteous and respectful atmosphere that makes it possible for people to listen to one another. This is simply good strategy. But if Francis, unlike the apologetic preachers, does not proclaim the Christian truth straightaway in an aggressive manner (*agredior*) and does not try to corner them with all kinds of apologetic arguments, his approach is not so much due to

---

[37] The full text is: *Agredior, inquam vos [Saracenos], non, ut nostri saepe faciunt, armis, sed verbis, non vi, sed ratione, non odio, sed amore*. Petrus Venerabilis, *Adversus nefandam sectam Saracenorum libri duo*. PL 189, 673. See James Kritzeck, *Peter the Venerable and Islam* (Princeton: Princeton University Press, 1964). In his book *Die Funktion der franziskanischen Bewegung in der Kirche. Eine pastoraltheologische Interpretation der grundlegenden franziskanischen Texte* (Schwyz, CH: Tau-Verlag, 1977), 165-67, Anton Rotzetter sees Peter the Venerable as a forerunner of Francis. In my view, however, there are fundamental differences between their approaches. Peter speaks about *agredior*, while Francis insists on *spiritualiter conversari inter*. Further Peter relies on words (*verba*) and reason (*ratio*) while Francis wishes his brothers to show they are Christians through their deeds (*opera*), and very specially through their being subject (*subditi*). See further in the text.

[38] The Latin word *conversari* suggests already an exchange, a "conversation" between the brothers and the Saracens. In more modern terms, *conversari* suggests a dialogue, rather than the monologue of the preacher.

strategic considerations of how best to capture the heart and mind of the Saracens,[39] but rather the result of his theological vision as it has grown in the course of years thanks to his commitment to follow "the humility and poverty of our Lord Jesus" (ER 9,1). Or, as he counsels his brothers who go among the Saracens, do whatever you do in their midst "for God's sake" (ER 16:6).

Subject to every human creature for God's sake

And it is this God who is "humility" (PrsG 4), Who calls Francis and his brothers, before everything else, also before they start preaching, "to be subject to every human creature for God's sake" (ER 16:6). This call is fully in line with the advise in the next chapter of the *Earlier Rule*, namely, that "all the brothers should preach by their deeds" (17:3). In other words, the truth with regard to God is first and foremost a truth to be done! It is the lived truth, and this alone, that really counts. For Francis it is then also quite obvious that living the truth of God's humility is the first way for the brothers to be present among the Saracens. By being present in this way through solidarity of service they "witness that they are Christians" (16:6), and, so I may add, not crusaders! And as Francis's advice clearly implies, in the lived truth of God's humility there is room for "every human creature."

---

[39] Here lies a great difference, for example, with recent discussions among church officials about the document *Ad catholicam. Responses to Some Questions Regarding Certain Aspects of the Doctrine on the Church*, issued by the Congregation for the Doctrine of the Faith on June 29, 2007. For their discussions are more about strategy than about theology. The document states that the one church of Christ is only to be found in the Roman Catholic Church. This statement provoked strong negative reactions from the churches of the Reformation. In a reply the Congregation defended itself by pointing out that it was an internal document! However, there were also critical observations of the German cardinals Lehmann and Kasper. The latter declared before other cardinals that it would have been better if the form, language and presentation of such documents were revised. In other words, not the content, only the strategy needs to be adapted and be brought up to date. The reactions of the other churches did not lead them to asking questions about their present doctrinal position and to develop a new theological vision. How, for example, do we theologically interpret the actual existence, for almost five centuries, of the churches of the Reformation and other ecclesial communities, especially since it is acknowledged that the Spirit of God is actively present and working among them? Or to what unity does the truth about God and about Jesus Christ call the churches, especially also since truth is essentially conditioned by time and place?

Faithful to the truth in a spirit of hospitality

Francis's faithfulness to this truth is therefore in the practice of everyday life always accompanied by a true spirit of hospitality. In this Francis differed radically from the world around him where the defense of the truth, just like the defense of any other possession, led religious authorities, often in collaboration with the temporal powers, to condemn and exclude the "other" or even worse.[40] There is nothing of condemnation in Francis's approach. In fact, whereas around him the language of condemnation and vilification, of hatred and violence abounded, even in the church's prayer, there is no trace of such language to be found in Francis's writings. Rather the opposite is true, as we will see. Living God's truth made Francis extend a hearty welcome to the other. Here I wish briefly to recall the beautiful story in the *Assisi Compilation* 115 about the robbers near the hermitage of Borgo San Sepolcro. In this story Francis advises his brothers to go into the forest, "spread out a table cloth on the ground, place bread and wine on it, and humbly and joyfully wait on the robbers while they are eating." Whomever they meet, the brothers should never approach them with power which divides and excludes. They are rather to deal with all people they meet – also the Saracens! – in a spirit of solidarity and service in order to make the community of all human creatures, willed by God, come true around the one and only table of the Lord. From this table no one is excluded, whether "friend or foe, thief or robber" (ER 7:14). Around this table, all wish one another the peace of the Lord (Test 22-23).

AN ASIAN PERSPECTIVE

Solidarity through service and building a peaceful society is also the wish of the Asian bishops. At various meetings of their Federation of Asian Bishops' Conference they have called the faithful, often just constituting a small minority among people of other faiths – Hinduism, Buddhism, Islam – to become a servant church which commits itself

---

[40] I need only to recall here the very violent crusade, started by Innocent III in 1208, against the Cathari (Albigensians) in Southern France, which lasted for twenty years.

to promote the Kingdom of God, the Kingdom of justice and peace, in this world, together with all people of good will in whose endeavors to lead a good life the church acknowledges the active presence of the Holy Spirit. Rather than an ecclesio-centric, or even a Christo-centric approach, the churches in Asia and their bishops favor thus a so-called regno-centric or kingdom centered approach to mission and dialogue. Central authorities often frowned upon this vision.[41] Rather than a servant church which sees its special calling in its historical context to cooperate with all to promote the values of justice and peace for all, the central authorities place in all their recent documents great emphasis on a church that proclaims the truth of the Christian faith, thereby often invoking the text of St. Paul: "Woe to me if I do not preach the gospel" (1Cor 9:16).[42] This text is not to be found in the writings of

---

[41] The declaration *Dominus Jesus* (2000), referring to bishops and theologians who defend this view, describes them as follows: "They stress the image of a church which is not concerned about herself, but which is totally concerned with bearing witness to and serving the kingdom. It is a 'Church for others,' just as Christ is the 'man for others.'" The declaration then continues in a rather strange and, in my mind, even unfair way, given the fact that it is speaking here about people who, inspired by the person and example of Jesus Christ, have committed themselves to the establishment of God's kingdom of liberation, when it quotes extensively from John Paul II's encyclical *Redemptoris missio* 17 (1991): "Together with positive aspects, these conceptions often reveal negative aspects as well. First, they are silent about Christ: the kingdom of which they speak is 'theo-centrically' based, since, according to them, Christ cannot be understood by those who lack Christian faith, whereas different people, cultures, and religions are capable of finding common ground in the one divine reality, by whatsoever name it is called. For the same reason, they put great stress on the mystery of creation, which is reflected in the diversity of cultures and beliefs, but they keep silent about the mystery of redemption. Furthermore, the kingdom, as they understand it, ends up either leaving very little room for the Church or undervaluing the Church in reaction to a presumed (sic) 'ecclesio-centrism' of the past and because they consider the Church herself only as a sign, for that matter a sign not without ambiguity." After this quote, the declaration concludes: "These theses are contrary to the Catholic faith because they deny the unicity of the relationship which Christ and the Church have with the kingdom of God" (19). For a further explanation of the theological background and meaning of these approaches, see my *Francis and Islam*, 161-86. It is particularly interesting to see how the kingdom centered approach originated in a very attentive reading of the prominent signs of the time on the Asian continent, namely, Asia's religiosity and poverty.

[42] I limit myself to two recent documents: the Declaration *Dominus Jesus* (August 6, 2000) and the very recent *Doctrinal Note on Some Aspects of Evangelization* (December 3, 2007) as I consider them representative of the church's official understanding of mission and dialogue. The text of Paul is quoted in *Dominus Jesus* 2, and in Doctrinal Note 2.

Francis.[43] The same holds true for another often quoted text, namely that of Jesus' missionary mandate in the gospel of Matthew: "Go and teach all nations" (Matt 28:18).[44] When Francis and his brothers choose a gospel text to open the chapter on mission, it is quite a different text from the same gospel of Matthew: "See, I am sending you like sheep in the midst of wolves" (10:16). Wolves, wild beasts: a common mocking name for the Saracens at that time, used also in papal documents, like the encyclical *Vineam Domini* of Innocent III, issued in April 1213. However, when Francis wrote chapter 16 of the *Earlier Rule* after his return from his visit to the sultan, he had discovered that the Saracens he had met were not wolves at all, but people of deep faith among whom the brothers should be present in solidarity and service, just as among all other people.

'When they see that it pleases the Lord'

But what is then the place of preaching in Francis's approach to the Saracens? When Francis believes in Jesus, the way, the truth and the life, it seems rather obvious that he cannot but also feel an urgent desire to convert the Saracens to accept this Jesus and his teaching. Or is there something else, something or rather someone higher? Francis writes that the brothers, as a second way of presence in the Muslim world, may preach to the Saracens "when they see that it pleases God" (ER 16:7). Two observations on this text are important. First, preaching comes in second place after the presence of the brothers as Christians, as disciples of the humble Jesus, among the Saracens.[45] Next, and

---

[43] "Woe" texts can be found in Adm 19:3; 20:3; 21:2; 26:2 and ER 21:8. However, they have no connection with 1Cor 9:16. One could even argue, somewhat mischievously, on the ground of attitudes developing among learned preachers that Francis's "woes" are directed to preachers, rather than to non-preachers.

[44] It is this text which, together with Mark 16:15-16: "Go out into the whole world and preach the gospel to every creature. He who believes and is baptized will be saved, but he who does not believe will be condemned," is quoted in the opening paragraph of both documents. Matthew's text is further also quoted in the conclusion of *Dominus Jesus* (23). It serves there as a kind of *inclusio* (concluding clasp) which repeats and thereby underlines the main theme of the declaration.

[45] This may come as a surprise to people whose image of Francis has been influenced by the story of Celano about Francis who, after hearing the gospel "about how the Lord sent out his disciples to preach, ... hastened to implement these words" and straightaway "began to preach penance to all with a fervent spirit and joyful attitude"

even more important is that it is not their own desire to preach and eventually to convert the Saracens that is to determine their actions, but God's pleasure, God's will, which often proves to be quite different from people's wishes and desires. Yet, with full confidence, the brothers can leave the decision in this matter to God's pleasure, trusting that God, who is the source of love and of all good, in God's own inscrutable ways will see to the salvation of all people, the Saracens included. And if God appears not to show any haste, as it seems to be the case with the Saracens, Francis is ready to wait patiently for God to act in God's own time, while at the same time continuing to live the truth of God's humility by showing his solidarity with the Saracens and serving them as best and as lovingly as he can.[46]

(1C 22-23). Or by the fact that many scholars categorize Francis and his brothers as wandering preachers (*Wanderprediger*). But is this image correct when we examine it in light of Francis's writings? It is most remarkable that Francis and his brothers in ER 14, where they speak about how the brothers are to go through the world, refer to the missionary discourses in the gospel of Luke, but do not mention preaching at all. If preaching were a defining characteristic of the brotherhood, would Francis and his brothers not have mentioned this? See Dino Dozzi, *Il Vangelo nella Regola non bollata di Francesco d'Assisi* (Rome: Istituto Storico dei Cappuccini, 1989), 211-12. Instead, Francis and his brothers state explicitly that the brothers have to wish the people whose houses they enter to work, the peace of the Lord. The same observation can be made regarding the way Francis describes the early beginnings of the brotherhood in his *Testament* 16-23. He refers to being subject to all, to manual work, to wages, to begging and sitting at the table of the Lord, and to the greeting of peace that the Lord had revealed to him, but he does not mention a single word about preaching nor does he give even the slightest hint. This is not to deny that the brothers at times may have exhorted people. However, it was not preaching, but rather doing penance that was uppermost on their mind. "The Lord gave me, brother Francis, thus to begin doing penance" (Test 1). A better name for the brothers would then also be: "wandering penitents" or, more specifically, "wandering peacemakers." See my *Francis and Islam*, 56-58, and my more recent "Francis' understanding of mission. Living the gospel, going through the world, bringing peace," in *Zeitschrift fur Missionswissenschaft und Religionswissenschaft* 92 (2008): 280-297. A further intriguing text in this connection is 2LtF 53. See below note 58.

A recent example of what I call clerical "eisegesis" is a publication by Pietro Messa in which he discusses an early problem of Francis and his brothers, referred to in 1C 35, namely: *utrum inter homines conversari deberent, an ad loca solitaria se conferre*, and to which he gave the title *Frate Francesco tra vita eremitica e predicazione* (Assisi: Edizioni Porziuncola, 2001). I fail to see how *inter homines conversari* can possibly be equated with *praedicatio*, a word that in 1C 35, in the formulation of the problem Francis and his brothers were facing, does not occur at all.

[46] It is particularly the non-Franciscan sources about Francis's visit to the sultan which stress that Francis went on a preaching mission. What other mission could he,

Do not want them to be different

This trust in God, leaving everything to God's pleasure, holds a very prominent place in Francis's life and spirituality. It is in a most revealing manner described at the beginning of the *Letter to a Minister* where Francis counsels a minister:

> [W]hoever has become an impediment to you [to love God], whether brothers or others, even if they lay hands on you, you must consider as grace. And you should want it to be this way and not otherwise.... And love those who do these things to you ... and do not wish them to be better Christians (2-7).

In other words, do not want people to be different from the way they present themselves in your life. Rather, since your life is in the hands of a good and loving God, you must look even at their seemingly harmful presence as a grace, as a God-given favor that cannot possibly form a hindrance to your love of God. On the contrary, if accepted, you show that you are truly obedient to God's loving will, which only desires what is good for you, and which will without fail lead you to life![47]

---

according to James of Vitry and Ernoul, a French crusade chronicler, possibly have had in mind when going to the Saracens? For in the crusaders' mentality religious had to take part in the crusade by attacking the Muslims, not with arms, but with words! I think, therefore, that James and Ernoul's account of Francis's meeting with the sultan has been strongly influenced by their crusader's bias. Just as the emphasis on Francis's desire for martyrdom in the Franciscan sources appears to point to a special bias of Franciscan authors. See my *Francis and Islam*, 58.

[47] At the beginning of ER 22 Francis expresses the same idea when he invites his brothers to follow Jesus' example and to call those their friends who "unjustly inflict distress and anguish, shame and injury, sorrow and punishment, martyrdom and death" on them (1-4). Francis felt very deeply about this, which explains also why, at the end of his life, he "strictly commands all the brothers through obedience ... not to dare ask any letter from the Roman Curia ... under the pretext ... of [preventing] the persecution of their bodies" (Test 25). This does not mean that they have to seek persecution, as is clear from the next verse: "But, wherever they are not received, let them flee into another country to do penance with the blessing of God" (Test 26; cf. ER 16:14). However, when persecution comes their way, they have to accept it as a blessing (ER 16:12). In ER 10:3-4 Francis applies the same idea to the sick brothers when he "begs them to thank God for everything and to desire to be whatever the Lord wills, whether sick or well."

Trust in the Lord

Also interesting in this context is a story in the *Assisi Compilation* 106, where Francis is questioned by one of his companions why he "tolerates" those brothers who do not observe the Rule, and does not "correct" them. Francis answers that he does not feel himself called "to become an executioner who beats and scourges the brothers, like a power in the world," to make them toe the line. Rather, he will try to overcome their vices and correct their behavior by word and example. And for the rest, Francis says, "I trust in the Lord."[48] However much Francis loves God and wishes people to follow the example of Jesus, who for him is the true way to life, yet a real drive to convert people and to make them different appears to be absent from Francis's mind. He trusts that whatever God in God's own time pleases to do with him and his brothers as part of God's patient dealings with humankind, is done well.[49]

You are patience

In Francis's approach to sinners and persecutors as described above we see various glimpses of that other name of God that I consider important to understand Francis's view on Islam: God is patience (PrsG 4). But whereas humility as name of God probably emerged rather early in the development of the brotherhood when it reflected on its socio-economic place in the world of Assisi where the brothers were confronted with the evils brought about by power and possessions, the definitive breakthrough of patience as name of God appears to be of a later date and has probably been strongly influenced by Francis's expe-

---

[48] It may be noticed that, in developing its story, AC 106 presents the popular view that God at times uses the devil as "the Lord's police" (*castaldi Domini*). A similar idea is also found in 2C 119-120. However, in retelling Celano's story, Bonaventure, the theologian, appears to have a problem with this popular view and hence omits any reference to the devil as the Lord's police. See my "Francis and the Devil. About the Devil in Francis' Writings, in the Opus Celanense, and in Franciscan Art," in *Verum, Pulchrum et Bonum. Miscellanea di studi offerti a Servus Gieben in occasione del suo 80° compleanno* (Rome, 2006), 97-153, here 129 and 142.

[49] This idea plays also an important role in Francis's repeated admonition that the brothers "must be careful not to be angry or disturbed at the sin of another, for anger and disturbance impede charity in themselves and in others" (LR 7:3; cf. Adm 11:2-3; ER 5:7; 11:4; 2 LtF 44).

riences, or rather his discoveries, during his stay among the Muslims and his reflection on these experiences, even after his return to Italy. But before I turn to this topic, I want to place this reflection on God as patience within the broader context of the Christian tradition that is quite familiar with this name, especially in its scriptures rather than in its patristic and medieval writings. In this way I hope to develop a better perspective on the significance of Francis's inclusion of patience as a name of God in his Praises of God, especially in relation to his understanding of Islam within the context of salvation history.

Patience – the biblical tradition

In Latin, the word *patientia* is used to translate two Greek words. The first word is *makrothymia*, longanimity. It refers to an attribute, a characteristic of God who, torn between punishment and forgiveness, is slow to anger and rather tolerates the individual and collective sins of his people while awaiting their conversion (Ex 34:6; Num 14:18; Ps 7:12; 85:15; 144:8). It is often accompanied by qualifications that underline God's tenderness, pity, indulgence, and fidelity. In the New Testament God's *patientia* is mentioned in Matt 18:26: Luke 18:7; Rom 2:4; 9:22; 1 Peter 3:20. It is inherited by Christ: 1 Tim 1:16; 2 Peter 3:9-15; and to be imitated by those who believe in God and in Christ: Matt 18:23-35; 1 Tim 1:16; James 5:7-8. The second word is *hypomonè*, which means: to sustain patiently, to endure, to persevere, often connected with an attitude of hopeful expectation. It refers always to a human virtue and is translated in various ways. The term *patientia* and its derivatives occur in Ps 9:19; 61:6; 70:5, but very frequently in the letters of the New Testament, stressing the need to patiently endure whatever sufferings the followers of Jesus may incur because of their allegiance to Jesus: Rom 5:3-5; 12:11-12; 2 Cor 6:4-6; 2 Thes 1:4-5; 2 Tim 3:10-12; Hebr 10:35-36; 12:1-2; 1 Peter 2:19-20; James 1:3-4; 5:10-11.[50]

---

[50] I owe this survey and other data to Michel Spanneut, "Patience," in *Dictionnaire de Spiritualité*, Vol. 12 (Paris: Beauchesne, 1984), 438-76, here 439-42.

The patristic and medieval tradition

Patientia as an attribute, a characteristic of God largely disappears in the treatises on patience the early Fathers of the church, like Tertullian, Cyprian, Lactantius wrote in the third and fourth centuries. They strongly emphasize *patientia* as a human virtue. This is not surprising as they live and write at a time when the Christian community suffers frequent and severe persecutions. However, *patientia* is not only necessary to remain faithful to Christ in time of persecution, but also in ordinary daily life. For as Lactantius observes: a person's whole life is a *certamen*, where good is accompanied by evil, and every virtue implies a struggle. Patience is then also the main virtue, the greatest of all virtues.[51] Continuing within this tradition at a time when the persecutions have ended, Gregory the Great (†604) describes patience as the martyrdom of the non-persecuted, and as the root and guardian of all virtues.[52] Emphasizing patience as a human virtue, the interest in patience as an attribute of God disappears. In fact, it was denied, ever since Augustine (354-430) stressed that patience is a gift of God and that, therefore, it cannot in the same way be said that God is patience, as it is said: *Deus caritas est*.[53] Augustine's view is resumed by Peter Lombard (c.1100-1160) who, quoting Augustine, formulates the thesis that the saying: "You are my patience and hope," refers to God as cause. This does not hold good for the saying: God is love, which refers to the very essence of God.[54]

---

[51] *Divinae Institutiones* III, 29:16; IV, 26:27; V, 22:2; VI, 18:16. See Spanneut, "Patience," 443-44.

[52] *Homiliae in Evangelium*, II, 35, PL 76, 1261-1263. See Spanneut, "Patience," 449.

[53] Augustinus, *De Trinitate*, lib.15, cap. 17.

[54] *Quod non est dictum per causam illud: Deus caritas est; sicut illud: Tu es patientia mea, et spes mea*. Petrus Lombardus, *Libri IV Sententiarum*, I, 17:3. One of the main points in Peter's argument, following Augustine, is that Ps 71:5 (Vulgate 70) speaks of *patientia mea et spes mea*, whereas in 1 John 4:8 it is simply said: *Deus caritas est*. See also note 66.

Tu es patientia mea ...

The text: *Tu es patientia mea et spes mea*, taken from Ps 70:5 (Vulgate), is quoted by Francis in Psalm 12 of his Office of the Passion of the Lord (OfP 12:4).[55] This psalm is scheduled for the hour of None in the season of Advent and on all Sun- and Feastdays. A most remarkable feature of this Office is that it runs from Passion time via Easter to Advent and Christmas, whereas the ordinary Office of the breviary runs from the Advent and Christmas via the Lenten season to Easter and Pentecost. Francis's Office is therefore oriented towards Advent and Christmas.[56] It is an expression, all the year long, of Francis's deep and intense longing for the advent of God in Jesus, and this not as a past event, but as something he wishes to happen in the present: now. Or, as he writes in the longer version of the Letter to the Faithful,[57] he wishes that all of us, in the power of the Lord's Spirit, will persevere in doing penance, "being subject to every human creature for God's sake," and thus become "mothers [of Jesus, who] give birth to him through holy deeds" (*sancta operatio*; 2LtF 47, 53).[58] It is then our mission in the world to give Jesus a new historical existence and so to complete Jesus' mission of liberation and redemption. And just as Jesus met with misunderstanding from his own disciples, and with opposition from

---

[55] I use the name given to this writing in the new English translation. A better name would be: Office of the Mysteries of the Lord. See Laurent Gallant and Andre Cirino, *The Geste of the Great King Office of the Passion of Francis of Assisi* (St. Bonaventure, NY: Franciscan Institute Publications, 2001), 202-03.

[56] See Friedrich Doormann, "In Jesus Christus solidarisch mit den Armen den Adventus Gottes erwarten. Ein basileia-theologicher Interpretationsansatz für das Passionsoffizium des heiligen Franziskus," in *Wissenschaft und Weisheit* 67 (2004): 191-203, here 192.

[57] I agree with Michael Cusato ("To Do Penance," 5-6, note 7) that the shorter version of the Letter to all the Faithful is distilled from the longer version. I am not so sure, however, that this was done by Francis and that both texts are to be dated between 1220 and 1221. I think there are strong indications that the shorter version is the work of a secretary and may even have been made after Francis's death.

[58] In the context of the previous discussion on preaching, it may be interesting to refer to the difference between Francis's interpretation with its stress on *sancta operatio* and the interpretation of *Glossa ordinaria* in its gloss on Matt 12:50: *Hi sunt mater mea, qui in credentium cordibus generant ... mater praedicando*, PL 114, 129. See Gerard Pieter Freeman, *Gelukkig wie in Jezus' voetspoor gaat. Een historisch kommentaar op de twee redakties van de 'Brief aan de Gelovigen' van Franciskus van Assisi* (Utrecht: Doctoral Dissertation, 1981), 105. The gloss goes back to Gregory the Great's *Homiliae in Evangelia*, III (*PL* 76, 1086).

some of the leaders of his own people, and in the end suffered condemnation and death, so also his followers will have to be prepared to undergo the same fate and to approach it in the same way as Jesus did: with patience.[59] Francis prayerfully addresses such an adverse situation in OfP 12 and in the preceding OfP 11. In these psalms he repeatedly refers to distress and trials (11, 1, 7-8; 12, 8-9), and prays that the Lord may give those who suffer, patience (12,4) so that they may endure whatever adversity they meet on their way.

... *spes mea, susceptor meus et refugium meum*

At the same time Francis prays for hope (12:4) so that the brothers, while patiently enduring their difficult and painful situation, may continue to place all their trust in the Lord, their guard and refuge (*susceptor meus et refugium meum*, 11:8; 12:9). Remarkable indeed is the number of other expressions Francis uses in these psalms, often more than once, to indicate that, despite all afflictions, people can rely on the Lord: their *adiutor; protector; locus munitus*.[60] All these expressions underline Francis's profound conviction, emphasized at the end of both OfP 6:16 and 7:11: "We *know* that the Lord has come and will come to give justice its rightful place."[61] This does not mean that people should passively undergo things. On the contrary, they should continue to carry out their own responsibilities with perseverance, that is, they should "take up their bodies and carry [Jesus'] holy cross and follow his most holy commands even to the end" (OfP 7:8), patiently waiting

---

[59] ... *patientiam, per quam in Christo manemus, ut venire cum Christo ad Deum possimus* ... Cyprian, *De bono patientiae*, PL 4, 634.

[60] Unfortunately, the new English translation does not seem to acknowledge here all the nuances of the Latin original.

[61] The Latin text has here *Et scimus, quoniam venit, quoniam veniet iustitiam iudicare*. In the new English translation this sentence is translated as follows: "And we know that he is coming, that he will come to judge justice." I follow here the new Dutch translation that reads: "Ja, wij weten dat hij gekomen is en komen zal om recht te doen aan gerechtigheid." *Franciscus van Assisi, De Geschriften* (Haarlem: Gottmer, 2004), 200-01. The justice Francis talks about is first and foremost the justice of the Kingdom (RH 3), on account of which Jesus' followers suffer persecution (ER 16:12; LR 10:11) and which Jesus acquired for the poor when he restored to them "alms as a legacy and a right due to them" (ER 9:8).

in the meantime for the coming of the Lord who will certainly come but at his own appointed time.[62]

The awakening of an insight

With his prayer in Psalm 12 of his Office Francis clearly stands within the tradition of *patientia* as it developed within the Christian community since the early ages: *patientia* is seen as a human virtue, a human strength, given by God to empower God's people in its struggles to remain faithful to Christ and his mission. The influence of this tradition can also easily be traced in other places in Francis' writings.[63] But then, rather surprisingly against this traditional background, Francis introduces *patientia* as a name of God in his Praises of God. In light of our starting principle that all God-talk is historical, conditioned by time and place, it is evident that the surprising introduction of this name of God finds its origin in the historical context of Francis's life. We mentioned already that on several occasions, as for example in his *Letter to a Minister*, Francis advised his brothers to set aside their own ideas and wishes that a troublesome brother be different, and to leave everything in the hands of God even when God's plans did not run parallel with theirs. This trustful attitude led Francis also, after the Lord had brought him among the Saracens, to advise his brothers not to start preaching until they had seen that it was in accordance with

---

[62] Or as Francis writes precisely at the end of ER 16, combining two different gospel texts: "You will possess your souls in patience (Luke 21:19); and whoever perseveres to the end, will be saved" (Matt 10:22; 24:13).

[63] See LR 10:9, where patience in persecution and sickness is recommended together with love for the persecutors – the combination of patience and love of one's enemies in a spirit of non-violence is already found in the early Latin church fathers (see Spanneut, "Patience," 444-46); Adm 13:2 where patience proves itself in times of adversity; Adm. 27:2, where patience prevents a person from getting angry or being disturbed (see also note 49). Interesting in several of these texts from Francis's writings is the pairing of patience and humility. This occurs already in Cyprian's *De bono patientiae* 2, and in the monastic tradition, for example, in John Cassian's *Institutiones* 4, 3:1; 4, 36:2; 6, 15:1; 7, 31; and the *Rule of Benedict*, 7:35-36 and 42 (Spanneut, "Patience," 443; 450). I have not been able to study this further and to find out whether this throws any light on the fact that in his *Praises of God* Francis mentions patience immediately after humility. In light of the fact that the traditional pair of humility and patience refers to human virtues, whereas the praises of God speak about humility and patience as divine names that Francis discovered at different times and in different places, I am inclined to conclude that there is no real connection between the two.

God's pleasure. In this advice of Francis we saw glimpses of an awakening insight in the mystery of God who is patience, is not hasty and acts according to his own pleasure that surpasses all our understanding: an insight that is not yet articulated there. Rather, even at the beginning of his stay among the Saracens, *patientia* as a human virtue must have been foremost in his mind as Francis tried to live among the Saracens in the spirit of Jesus. For the service of wounded Saracens and captured crusaders was hard and difficult under the burning sun in the mosquito-infected Nile delta; he suffered hunger and thirst and his peaceful intentions were at times misunderstood. To endure all this and to persevere in doing good in these adverse circumstances, Francis must have often prayed to the Lord to grant him patience.

The breakthrough

This situation changed thoroughly when Francis at his new place discovered that the Saracens were quite different from the cruel, unbelieving infidels that crusade preaching and propaganda had made them out to be. Gradually, Francis was deeply impressed by their regular and devout prayer to which they were publicly called five times a day. He admired the great respect they had for their holy book, the Koran, God's written word among them. He was inspired by their reverence for the holy names of Allah which they continually recited while letting the chain of beads quietly pass through their fingers. But more than by these external religious practices, Francis was moved by their deep attitude of faith, by their total surrender, their radical submission, their unconditional obedience to the will of Allah (*islam*) which were the source of these practices. To please God and God alone was their only aim in life. These discoveries gave him not only a radically different impression of the Saracens. They also confronted him, more forcefully than ever before, with the question: why? Why does God keep delaying the conversion of these God-fearing people? Why doesn't it seem to please God to open their hearts and minds for the message of Jesus? Prayerfully reflecting on these questions, in the light of his faith in a good and loving God whose gracious presence he had observed among the Saracens, Francis sought to understand what God was revealing to him in and through these new discoveries.[64] Trying to read these God-given signs of the time, all his past and present experiences came together and a new insight, a new knowledge dawned upon him. Until then it had been slumbering at the back of his mind but now it was becoming ever clearer that in his dealings with humankind God acts radically different from the way people act. Once among the Muslims, people like James of Vitry did not want to wait but, impatiently and hastily, rushed to convert the Muslims, for their salvation was at stake. Their efforts, though, met with little or no success at all. It made Francis think. Apparently God followed quite a different approach. God seemed to show no haste and appeared even not to be overly concerned about a delay in the conversion of the Muslims.[65] Yet at the same time Francis noticed to his great amazement that God was all the time actively present and working among the Muslims. God had not forgotten them or excluded them, or written them off. God was interested in them, but evidently acted according to his own timetable and knew to wait for the realization of his plans: plans that were always concerned with the life of the people God had created. In one word, God clearly had patience with the Saracens. Having made this discovery at his new place among the Muslims, this new insight continued to work on his mind until it found its articulation four years later in the *Praises of God*: God, You are *patientia*, patience.[66]

The climax of a learning process

This rediscovered name of God formed the climax of a learning process that started when God inspired Francis to go among the Sara-

---

[64] The importance of God's revelation in the events of his life is strongly emphasized in the seven "revelatory" interventions of God which Francis mentions in his *Testament*. In vv. 1-23 he briefly recalls how the Lord intervened at decisive moments in his life, from the time of his conversion till the arrival of the first brothers: 1, 2, 4, 6, 14 (2x), 23.

[65] The problem of the "delay of God" surfaces in the Gospel, for example, in the parable of the wheat and the weeds (Matt 13:24-30) and in Jesus' saying that "the Father in heaven makes the sun rise on the evil and the good, and lets rain fall on the just and on the unjust" (Matt 5:45). However, the word *patientia* does not occur here. In the passages where *patientia* occurs in the Letter to the Romans, there is always question of a "delay."

[66] Remarkable is that in the *Praises of God* the possessive pronoun *mea* is omitted in the case of *patientia*, while it has been maintained in the case of *spes*. See note 54.

cens, and that now was bearing fruit after a long and prayerful reflection on all the wonderful things that had happened to him in their midst, and in and through which God revealed to him the mystery of who God is. Like the name, All-powerful, is a name of God within the Christian tradition which Francis became more aware of during his stay among the Saracens, so also the name of God who is patience originated within Francis's Christian tradition of faith but received a new dimension, a new depth in his contacts with Islam. We do not know whether Francis was familiar with the ninety-nine most beautiful names of Allah, and especially with the last name: *As-Shabur*, the Patient, the Timeless One.[67] But, as we mentioned earlier, Francis was definitely influenced during his learning process by his growing awareness of God's gracious presence among the Muslims in their total submission and obedience to the will of Allah, to Allah's pleasure.[68] Observing God's presence among them made it possible for Francis to give a positive turn to God's delay. Having gone among the Muslims to be subject to them for God's sake and to bring them the peace of Jesus, Francis had not excluded the possibility of actively working towards their conversion, but he learned that he should not engage in preaching activities except when he saw that it was pleasing to God. God's pleasure which he had always sought to fulfill in his life, became an even stronger motive for his actions once he got a deeper insight in *islam*.[69] And if it pleased God to delay, he was now ready to see this delay as a God-given sign that he had to read carefully in order to be able to truly submit himself to the will of God who is patience.

---

[67] Besides listing patience among the names of Allah, Muslims also strongly emphasize the human virtue of patience in consonance with the Koran, sura 2:177; 3:17, 120, 186, 200; 10:109; 11:49, 115; 13:24; 16:127; 18:28; 20:130; 23:111; 25:75; 28: 80; 30:60; 40:55, 77; 46:35; 50:39; 70:5; 73:10; 74:7; 90:17; 103:3.

[68] The deep admiration and appreciation Francis had for the Islam, may also have influenced him when writing his Letter to all the Brothers (Letter to the Entire Order). For this letter, as observed earlier, shows various signs of Islamic influence, is really a letter on obedience, as its introduction (5-11) clearly shows. Moreover the corpus of the letter ends with a kind of final exclamation mark in v. 46, where Francis refers to the example of Jesus who "gave his life that he would not lose the obedience of his most holy Father." See my "Francis' Letter to all the Brothers," 16-20, 71-72.

[69] "Pleasing" God and God alone is prominently present in "Francis's Letter to all the Brothers": vv. 15, 42, 50. See the commentary on these verses in my "Francis' Letter to all the Brothers," 27-29, 77.

Some church documents

About twenty years ago, some implicit and explicit references to God-who-is-patience appeared in church documents. It happened for the first time during the much-publicized meeting John Paul II had with 80,000 young Muslims in the stadium of Casablanca (Morocco) on August 19, 1985. John Paul II, speaking about the fundamental differences between Islam and Christianity, observed that we have to accept them with humility, knowing that we find ourselves here in the presence of a mystery that will be fully revealed only at the end of time.[70] In the same year the Secretariat for non-Christians stated explicitly: "We live in the age of the patience of God for the church and every Christian community, for no one can oblige God to act more quickly than he has chosen to do."[71] And a few years later, in 1991, the Pontifical Council for Interreligious Dialogue and the Congregation for the Evangelization of Peoples jointly published the instruction: *Dialogue and Proclamation*, which states: "All, both Christians and the followers of other religious traditions, are invited by God to enter into the mystery of God's patience, as human beings seek God's light and truth. Only God knows the times and stages of the fulfillment of this long human quest."[72] Unfortunately, no reference whatsoever to the idea of living in the age of God's patience or of entering into the mystery of God's patience can be found any longer in the more recent declaration *Dominus Jesus* or in the *Doctrinal note*, even though *Dominus Jesus* does quote the instruction *Dialogue and Proclamation*. It is clear that a different wind is blowing in the Roman curia which started already in 1991 with the publication of John Paul's encyclical *Redemptoris missio*.

A different Francis

After this short intermezzo I return again to Francis. Whenever he entered a new situation, Francis had always done so with a free and open mind, always ready to learn whatever God wanted to reveal to

---

[70] For the text of the Pope's address, see: Maurice Borrmans, "Le discours de Jean-Paul II aux jeunes de Casablanca," in *Seminarium* 26 (1986): 44-72, here 57.

[71] "The Attitude of the Church towards the Followers of Other Religions. Reflections and Orientations on Dialogue and Mission," in *Bulletin* 56 (1985): 141.

[72] *Bulletin* 77 (1991): 248-49.

him. And so it was also after he had returned to Italy – an Italy that was no longer the same as before because he was no longer the same person as the one who had left for Egypt. With all his new discoveries fresh in his mind, Francis wanted to share them with clergy, civil authorities and people, as soon as he returned from the Middle East. And so Francis, "your servant and little one" (1 LtCus 1) starts writing short letters in which the discoveries he made play a prominent role. In his *Letter to the Clergy*[73] he urges all clerics to show reverence and respect, not only for "the most holy Body and Blood of our Lord Jesus Christ," his favorite expression – nowhere Francis uses the term "Eucharist" – but also for the Lord's "most holy written names and words" (LtCl 1:10-12; 1LtCus 2; Test 10-12). On his own Francis, thus, takes the initiative to complement the proposals of council and popes regarding the Eucharist in light of his personal experiences among the Saracens. Here Francis, the little one, shows an extraordinary consciousness of his mission. Apparently he is deeply convinced that the Lord did not reveal all these things to him during his stay among the Muslims in order to keep them for himself. No, whereas during his stay among the Saracens he had his reservations about preaching, he now knows clearly what pleases God. There is then also no hesitation whatsoever in Francis's mind as regards his mission and its urgency now that he is back in the Christian world. A clearly different Francis from the one who, in the *Earlier Rule* 16, advises his brothers not to preach to the Saracens except when they see that it pleases God.

A Muslim-Christian ecumenism in praising God

However, uppermost on Francis's mind is the question concerning the implications of his newly won insight in God's patience and, in light of this, of his positive interpretation of God's delay in converting the God-fearing Muslims. Seeing this delay as a God-given sign of the time, Francis interprets it as a call addressed to him not to intensify his preaching activities or those of his brothers to convert the Muslims.

---

[73] In the critical edition of Francis's writings, Esser argues that there are two versions of Francis's Letter to the Clergy. The editors of the new English translation follow his view. In a forthcoming article in *Franciscan Studies* I try to prove that Esser did make a mistake, especially where he argued in favor of a literary dependence of Francis's letter on the papal bull. A linguistic analysis of both documents shows, in my opinion, that such dependence does not exist.

Rather they are to devote themselves to bring Muslims and Christians together in prayer to the One, All-powerful God in whom both Muslims and Christians believe. To heed this call, knowing that this is what pleases the Lord, Francis feels the urge to write letters to the custodians and to the mayors and councilors of the cities. In those letters Francis urgently requests both ecclesiastical and civil authorities to make provisions so that people are called to prayer by a messenger "in such a way that praise and thanks may always be given to the all-powerful God by all people throughout the whole world" (1 LtCus 8; LtR 7).[74] In Francis's view, therefore, God, in God's divine pleasure, wishes that "all people throughout the whole world" – a world that for Francis includes the Saracens as well – commit themselves to a Christian-Muslim ecumenism in praising God.[75] In this *oikumene*, in this global house, Muslims and Christians are joined together in what for them as believing people is essential to their faith: to praise and thank God in prayer – a prayer which translates itself in deeds of submission, of obedience to God's will, to God's pleasure. Or, to say it in a more modern idiom – Francis views the existing religious pluralism not as a deficiency, as something negative, an evil which we have eradicate as soon as possible. Rather, he considers it as a fact, permitted by God, who is patience and who follows his own inscrutable ways, a fact therefore which we have to accept and to give a positive interpretation.

To compete in good works

A similar idea about the theological and practical significance of the actually existing pluralism of religions can also be found in the Koran. Thus in the context of the relation with Jews and Christians, the Koran states in *Sura* 5 (Medina): "Unto every one of you we have appointed a (different) law and way of life. And if God had so willed, he could surely have made you all one single community: but (he willed it

---

[74] A totally different, very negative view on the Muslim call to prayer can be found about a century later in canon 25 of the council of Vienne (1311-1312). For the text, which betrays a gross ignorance of Islam and the place of its prophet, see my *Francis and Islam*, 244-45, note 104.

[75] The expression "Christian-Muslim ecumenism in praising God" is borrowed from Leonhard Lehmann, "The two Letters of Saint Francis to the Custodians: Beginnings of a Christian-Muslim Ecumenism in Praising God," *Franciscan Digest* I,1 (May 1991): 21-56.

otherwise) in order to test you by means of what he has given you. Vie, then, with one another in doing good works! Unto God you all must return; and then he will make you truly understand all that on which you differed" (*Sura* 5:48).[76] A similar idea is also expressed at the end of *Sura* 10 (Mekka) where the Koran deals with the preaching mission of Jonah who was successful only in one city: "And if your Lord had willed, all who are on earth would have believed together. Would you then compel people to become believers? It is not for any soul to believe save by the permission of God" (*Sura* 10:99-100). See further *Sura* 35 (Mekka) which speaks about the last judgment and which is often quoted as the source for the name of Allah, the Patient One: "If God would punish the people for their sins, he would not have left a single creature on earth. But he gives them respite for a predetermined end-time. Once their end-time is fulfilled, God is seer of his servants" (*Sura* 35:45).

Vision of unity and peace

Looking in the mirror that is God and searching how to reflect the divine in relation to the Muslims, a vision of unity and solidarity gradually dawned on Francis – a vision in which Muslims and Christians vie with one another in good deeds, deeds of mutual service to each other or, as Francis would say, of "washing one another's feet" (ER 6:3; cf. John 13:14). According to some, this vision completely loses sight of the reality with all its oppositions, its tensions and enmities, and hence is very dangerous for the security of the Western world. We cannot, so they say, let the threat of terrorism go unanswered. I wholeheartedly disagree. For such a vision of being one humanity, of truly belonging together as members of the one human family, can inspire us, as it did Francis, to transcend all oppositions and divisions and to overcome the fear, greatly enhanced by the media, that our culture, the very basis of our society and its democratic institutions, is in danger of being overrun. And where such a fear paralyzes people or leads them to violent

---

[76] According to Maurice Borrmans, M.Afr., who was at that time director of the Pontificio Istituto di Studi Arabi e d'Islamistica (PISAI) in Rome and probably had a hand in writing the pope's address in Casablanca, John Paul II had this *Sura* in mind when he said that we have to accept the differences between Christianity and Islam with humility and to wait with patience till the end of time before the truth will be revealed. See note 70.

overreactions, such a vision offers us a truly counter-cultural counterweight and opens the way to a society where living the truth about God who is humility and patience, brings us all, "every human creature," together in a solidarity of service and hospitality, that leads to peace, and in the positive, grateful acceptance of the intentions which God, the Merciful, in God's divine pleasure has with the different religions. Peace and all good. *Assalamalaikum.*[77]

---

[77] I wish to extend my most sincere thanks to Michael F. Cusato, O.F.M. for inviting me to give the opening address at the Eighth Franciscan Forum and for his very helpful comments on an earlier version of this article; to Kathy Warren, O.S.F. the inspiring facilitator at the forum, for her intermediary role, for her constant readiness to answer my questions and her wonderful hospitality and friendship, and to Michael Blastic, O.F.M. the respondent to my address, for his appreciative and encouraging response.

Mirroring God: Metaphors of the Mirror in the Writings of Ibn Arabi and St. Clare of Assisi

F. Betul Cavdar

This paper consists of three parts: firstly, an introductory piece in which I try to clarify my understanding of the interfaith dialogue between Christianity and Islam; secondly, an elaboration of Clare of Assisi's usage of the mirror image; and thirdly, a concise look into Ibn Arabi's sophisticated theosophy and how he utilizes the mirror as a metaphor. In conclusion, I try to put St. Clare and Ibn Arabi into conversation by comparing their depictions of the perfect mirrors, Jesus in the case of Clare and Prophet Muhammad for Ibn Arabi. Consequently I indicate that although the mirrors they take as models are different, exemplary concepts and qualifications they see in these mirrors are not.

Clarifying the Methodology of Interfaith Writings

I have always found it quite challenging to establish links and find similarities between different religious traditions. For my academically trained mind, detecting differences rather than similarities has always been easier to do. Until recently I found studies of comparative religion rather superficial and unsatisfying. I wondered what the point was in such studies. My view slowly changed as I interacted more and more with a Christian audience as a religious studies student and scholar with a Muslim background. The interaction showed me that insiders always found their own religion more sensible and valuable while "the other" religion was often seen as strange and meaningless. In my case, I realized that in order to help my audience make sense of Islam, I had to put myself in their shoes and ask questions that would come to them instinctively. After a few experiences, it became clear that explaining a religion to an unfamiliar audience always had to start with pointing to similarities first and then aim at creating curiosity for more salient points.

Creating curiosity about another religion is not always an easy task. We all tend to classify religions under certain labels with which we are comfortable and feel the satisfaction of the controlled information. Most of the time, the religious tradition we belong to may already have produced polemical literature regarding the other religion and we cannot help but think in terms of this restrictive literature. The instructor or presenter of the religion, therefore, has to point to surprisingly diverse texts and figures within a particular religious tradition in order to challenge these restrictions and labels.

The two religions we want to bring into conversation today, Islam and Catholicism, share a long history of political adversity and polemical literature against each other. Therefore, for attempts of interfaith dialogue to be successful it is necessary that both sides make an effort to confront their prejudices against the other religion and make an honest attempt to understand and appreciate. For Christians, this effort entails reconsidering their image of Islam as a religion of violence and destruction that hopelessly missed the point when it denied the incarnation of Jesus Christ. On the other hand, Muslims have to take a look at their deep-seated rejection of the position of Jesus in the Christian tradition. Even though Islam, as a religion, has taken pride in its spotless monotheism for centuries, it is possible to develop a sense of the divine agent acting as an intermediary between the highest divine and the human being. Theologies of this sort, after all, are not totally extinct among various Islamic interpretations of the divine and the way God operates on the earth.

Although I see this appreciation for the other religion possible on a rhetorical level, I also realize that changing the formal theological stance towards the other religion is one of the hardest things to achieve. Therefore efforts of this kind – coming together as practitioners of different religions and discussing what our religion means for us and for those who came before us on a spiritual level – promise slow but exciting developments in the work of interfaith dialogue. After all, changes that start from the bottom and find their way up are always more influential and persistent than those imposed from the top down.

In that sense, this paper is a product of a Muslim trying to understand the spiritual experiences of Clare of Assisi and comparing them to those of Ibn Arabi. The challenge for me as the author is twofold. In the first part, I have to make sense of a religious text that has a very different context and language from that to which I am accustomed. In the second part, I have to make Ibn Arabi, whose writing is interfused with Quranic images, understandable for a Christian audience. It will inevitably pose certain challenges for me as I write it, and for you, as you strive to gain understanding.

One of the ways to overcome the challenging nature of writings from different faiths is to start from a common point shared by practitioners of both religions. For this paper the common point is the mirror imagery used both by Clare of Assisi and Ibn Arabi in their interpretation of the relationship between the human being and the divine. Although mirror imagery constituted a starting point for this paper, closer textual readings reveal more subtle common points that will be pointed out in the course of the paper.

Before beginning a detailed comparison, it is important to realize that mirror imagery is greatly indebted to the biblical tradition that accepts human beings as created in the image of God. This tradition, which both Christianity and Islam adopted from Judaism, places the human being in a position superior to the rest of the creation. The principle, of course, gains special dimensions in accordance with the theology each religion teaches. In Christianity, the incarnation of Jesus Christ is an indication of the value and significance human beings carry in the eyes of God. God's love for human beings is so vast that he is willing to send his own son among them. In Islamic tradition, on the other hand, this biblical principle is known in the form of a prophetic saying: God created Adam upon his own form (*ëala suratihi*). The idea is also supported by other prophetic sayings, a very famous one reads: He who knows himself (his soul) knows his Lord. Sufis abundantly use these kinds of references to describe the special link between the human being and the creator, and to draw attention to the need to search depths of human psyche.

Both Clare and Ibn Arabi are aware of the special position human beings are granted in their own religious traditions. In this context they demonstrate such similarity that when Clare mentions that "… the heavens and the rest of the creation cannot contain their Creator, and only the soul of a faithful person is his dwelling place and throne,"[1] she is, in fact, using a saying which is a favorite of Ibn Arabi. In its

---

[1] Joan Mueller, *Clare's Letters to Agnes, Texts and Sources* (St. Bonaventure, NY: The Franciscan Institute, 2001), 79.

well-known Islamic form the saying is recorded from the mouth of God: "My heavens and my earth embrace me not, but the heart of my believing servant does embrace me."[2] This shared saying demonstrates the unique capacity of the human heart as understood by these mystics and gives a clue regarding the roots which nourished mystical interpretations in both religions.

Clare of Assisi and Mirroring God

Clare was born at Assisi, Italy in 1193.[3] Her decision to lead a life devoted to the spiritual path came after she heard Saint Francis preach in her hometown. After a series of conversations between the two, Clare escaped her family house and joined the movement around Francis. For the rest of her life, Clare struggled to obtain papal recognition for the Franciscan way of life. Her attempts to make sure that the sisters living in her monastery would not be forced to accept material possessions were accepted by Pope Innocent IV in 1253, two days before she died.

Some of the most important material we have from Clare are her letters to Agnes of Prague (1211-1282). Agnes belonged to the royal family of Bohemia and was engaged to the German emperor Frederick II. When she chose to become a Franciscan as a young girl, her decision was not received well by his courtly family and she was under constant pressure to return to her previous lifestyle. In her letters to Agnes, Clare celebrates her dedication to the monastery and urges her to be an imitator of Christ in every aspect of her life. She also gives Agnes practical advice regarding prayer, rituals, and life in the monastery.

In Clare's letters to Agnes, Jesus Christ appears as the perfect mirror who is to be taken as a constant model. His perfection has two dimensions: his divinity and his humanity. In his divinity, Jesus is the perfect mirror of eternity and the perfect presentation of the divine Father. For Clare, experiencing God can only be achieved through his

---

[2] William Chittick, *The Sufi Path of Knowledge* (Albany, NY: The New York University Press, 1989), 107.

[3] Sources for Clare's life: *Francis and Clare: The Complete Works*, ed. Regis J. Armstrong and Ignatius C. Brady (New York: Paulist Press, 1982), 169-73; Mueller, *Clare's Letters to Agnes: Texts and Sources*; for a general understanding of St. Clare and her contemporary relevance see Ilia Delio, *Clare of Assisi: A Heart Full of Love* (Cincinnati: St. Anthony Messenger Press, 2007).

only accessible manifestation which happens to be Jesus Christ. As the sole knowable and understandable part of God, Jesus is also the one and only mirror of the divinity for human beings. Through his incarnation Jesus' human life presents the only possible way of transforming the self and "becoming like God." In his image taken as a mirror, Clare pictures Jesus on the cross sacrificing himself in poverty and humility. It is this poverty and humility, she admonishes Agnes, that she has to see in the mirror of her heart and imitate continually.

In her third letter, Clare uses the mirror imagery for the first time and urges Agnes to achieve transformation by placing her mind in "the mirror of eternity."

> Place your mind in the mirror of eternity; place your soul in the splendor of glory; place your heart in the figure of the divine substance; and through contemplation, transform your entire being into the image of the Divine One himself.[4]

Here Clare's attention is on the divine character of Jesus. She uses "the mirror of eternity," "the splendor of glory," and "the figure of the divine substance" interchangeably. Focused on the divinity of Jesus, Clare connects transformation of the self to the contemplation of Christ, but she does not say much with regard to the nature of this contemplation. It is exciting to see that, in her fourth letter, Clare develops the mirror imagery in a more detailed form and seems more fascinated with the human character of Jesus. In this letter, Clare urges Agnes to imagine Jesus Christ as her mirror and examine her face in this untarnished mirror everyday.

> ... [B]ecause the vision of him is (...) a mirror without tarnish. Look into this mirror everyday, O queen, spouse of Jesus Christ, and continually examine your face in it, so that in this way you may adorn yourself completely, inwardly and outwardly.... Moreover in this mirror shine blessed poverty, holy humility and charity beyond words, as you will be able to contemplate throughout the entire mirror.[5]

---

[4] *Clare's Letters to Agnes*, III: 12-14, 77.
[5] *Clare's Letters to Agnes*, IV: 14-18, 93-95.

Christ, for Clare, is the mirror without any tarnish. In his flawlessness, he is able to reflect the tiniest pieces of imperfection that might afflict the seeker of the divine. The imitator, therefore, always has to place Christ's reflection in front of oneself and study one's shortcomings in comparison to Christ. It is especially through his suffering that Christ shows the way to be the image of the divine. The virtues Clare mentions over and over – poverty, humility and charity – are reflected in the mirrored Christ throughout his life, starting from his being born in a manger in poverty and ending with his terrible death on the cross. The image of his body on the cross reflects how much sacrifice and suffering is to be endured in order to be the perfect mirror for all humanity. Humanity is as weak and desperate as he appeared on the cross, while divine love for humanity is as profound as this image indicates. Clare specifically advises Agnes to ponder his image on the cross more often than any other image:

> Indeed, ponder the final days of this mirrored one, contemplate the ineffable love with which he was willing to suffer on the tree of the cross and die there a kind of death that is more shameful than any other. That mirror suspended upon the wood of the cross there kept urging those passing by of what must be considered, saying: O all you who pass by this way, look and see if there is any suffering like my suffering.[6]

It is on the cross where the mirror character of Jesus becomes most apparent for Clare. In a strangely paradoxical sense, the immeasurable horror of this event makes it possible for Jesus to be the perfect mirror of love, poverty and humility. His powerless moment on the cross, while outwardly contradicting the divine character of Jesus, is the strongest presentation of the divinity for Clare. Clare even calls Jesus "the mirror on the cross" without feeling the need to mention his name. The mirror of the cross gives a message of self-sacrifice that would be only possible through such a horrible event. That is exactly why, for Clare, every Christian devoted to the spiritual path needs to reevaluate this moment at the cross over and over again, and see him asking "is there any suffering like my suffering?"

---

[6] *Clare's Letters to Agnes* IV: 23-25, 95-97.

Ibn Arabi and Mirroring God

Ibn Arabi (1165-1240) was born approximately thirty years before Saint Clare in Islamic Andalusia (Spain).[7] He belonged to an influential family and as a child and teen received the regular religious education of the time. The mystical visions he experienced as a seventeen-year-old led him to spend the rest of his life as a mystic who would repeatedly have mystical experiences. When he was thirty, he left Spain for Tunis, and then traveled to the East. After performing the pilgrimage in Mecca, he spent some years visiting several cities in Syria, Iraq, Egypt, and Turkey. During these visits, he became involved with different Sufi circles in each city he visited, and also acted as an advisor to the various caliphal courts. He permanently settled down in Damascus in 1223 and produced some of his most important writings during that time. Ibn Arabi was a very prolific writer to whom sources attribute up to eight hundred books most of which are short treatises. His main work, *Futuhat al-Makkiyya* (*The Meccan Openings*), is a large compendium of metaphysics, theology, cosmology and jurisprudence. His other important work, *Fusus al-Hikam* (*The Bezels of Wisdom*), is a more concise and accessible formation of his ideas and one of the most commented on books in the Islamic history.

Ibn Arabi left a deep and lasting mark on the mystical tradition of Islam and it is almost impossible to find a mystical trend that was not influenced by his ideas after the thirteenth century. Although his understanding of the divine and his relationship to the cosmos were unfamiliar to orthodox thinkers and created great controversy, and he was presented as an infidel, Ibn Arabi continued to be recognized as *al-Shaykh al-Akbar*, the greatest master, by his admirers. His captivating theosophy deeply influenced mystical philosophy, practice, poetry and prose particularly in Iran, Turkey and India.

The straightforward and simple writing of Clare is not characteristic of Ibn Arabi. He is notorious for his intimidating erudition, painstaking allegorical language and complex use of Arabic words. His theological and cosmological worldview with its subtle points is quite

---

[7] Sources for Ibn Arabi's life include Claude Addas, *The Quest for the Red Sulphure: The Life of Ibn Arabi* (Cambridge: Islamic Texts Society, 1993); Seyyed Hossein Nasr, *Three Muslim Sages* (Cambridge: Harvard University Press, 1964), 92-97; Chittick, *The Sufi Path of Knowledge*, x-xv.

difficult to grasp fully. Fortunately, interest in Ibn Arabi has increased immensely in academia in recent decades, and some very impressive works have appeared. This paper, in this sense, is especially indebted to the work of William Chittick who translated many parts from the voluminous *Futuhat al-Makkiyya* into English and successfully provided an overall view of Ibn Arabi's mystical thinking.

In order to make sense of Ibn Arabi's usage of the mirror as a metaphor that explains the relationship between the human being and God, it is important to be aware of two points concerning Islamic tradition that influenced Ibn Arabi. Firstly, although following the same pattern and idea, the Quranic creation story differs in some respects from the biblical one. In the Quran, the different and superior nature of Adam is explained through a conversation between God and the angels. According to these verses, angels, at first, protest against God's decision to create Adam claiming that the human being would only lead to mischief and blood. God, however, does not change his mind; he creates Adam and teaches him "the names." Afterwards Adam becomes able to cite the names of things, while angels cannot.

> When your Lord said to the angels: 'I am placing a deputy on earth,' they said: 'Will you place one who will make mischief in it and shed blood while we sing your praise and glorify your sanctity?' He said: 'I know what you do not know.' And he taught Adam all the names. Then he laid them before the angels. He said: 'Tell me the names of these if you are truthful.' They said: 'Glory be to you; we have no knowledge other than what you taught us. You are the All-knowing, the Wise.' He said: 'O Adam, tell them their names.' When Adam told them their names God said: 'Did I not tell you that I know the unseen in the heavens and the earth, and that I know what you reveal and what you conceal?' And he said to the angels: 'Prostrate yourselves before Adam,' they all prostrated themselves except the Satan ...[8]

As the verses indicate, after Adam is able to tell "the names," angels are asked to bow down before him. This unusual command caused

---

[8] Quran 2: 30-34, *The Qur'an: A Modern English Version*, trans. Majid Fakhry (Cleveland: Garnet Publishing, 1997).

many interpretations in Islamic exegesis, and for Ibn Arabi, the connection between "the names" and Adam's superiority over the angels is more complex than it seems at first sight. He explains that Adam's ability to tell the names should be understood in connection with the Quranic reference to the Names of God and their relationship to the cosmos.

In the Quran, the most beautiful names are said to belong to God. "And to Allah belong the most beautiful names; so call him by them"(Quran 7:180) instructs the Quran, while a prophetic tradition teaches that God's names are ninety-nine in number and promises heavenly rewards for those who recite them. Following this order, Sufis give special importance to the names of God and practice *dhikr*, the daily repetition of God's names in a particular manner. Although the number ninety-nine is well-known and established in Islamic circles, there has never been an agreement on exactly which names constitute this number. Some of the names that are mentioned frequently in the Quran – among others: the Living, the Powerful, the All-knowing, the All-seeing, the All-hearing, the Generous, the Glorious – are always part of the list, but for the rest different Muslim scholars suggest various classifications of the names.

Ibn Arabi, on the other hand, asserts that the names are in fact infinite in number, corresponding to the endless self-disclosures of the Divine that fill the universe.[9] In his thinking, God's names designate his essence, attributes and acts. While in his essence God is unknowable and without reference to anything else, through his relationship with the cosmos he acquires the names and qualities.[10] The fact that he created the universe, for example, provides him with the name "the Creator." In this sense, the cosmos – making possible for God to assume relationships – manifests/mirrors him. Each thing in the universe reflects some attributes of God passively, while certain names are reflected in certain objects actively. The sun, volcanoes, and oceans, for example, reflect the name "the Powerful" more actively than some other creatures. Things, however, do not have the capacity to manifest all of God's names in one instance, and hence arises the need for the creation of the human being.

---

[9] William Chittick, *Ibn Arabi: Heir to the Prophets* (Oxford: Oneworld Publications, 2005), 29.

[10] Chittick, *The Sufi Path of Knowledge*, 9.

In the first chapter of *Fusus al-Hikam*, Ibn Arabi focuses on the creation of Adam whom he sees as the archetype of humankind. Starting from the creation of the cosmos, he explains:

> The Reality (God) wanted to see the essences of his most beautiful names or to put it another way, to see his own essence, in an all-inclusive object encompassing the whole (divine) Command, which, (...) would reveal to him his own mystery. For the seeing of a thing, itself by itself, is not the same as its seeing itself in another, as it were in a mirror.[11]

The cosmos, then, is created because God desires to have a vision of his own mystery. Creation is the mirror that God employs to visualize his own self, and therefore the totality of creation does not have any reality beyond that of a reflection in the mirror. There is only the oneness of God, the only Real being, and anything other than Him is merely a reflection of Him.

In this sense, for Ibn Arabi, creation is the continual self-disclosure of God. Thus it is not appropriate to understand the creating act of God as an event that happened once-and-for-all in the past and is completed, but rather it is a continuous and ever-recurring process. In each moment God recreates and reveals himself in a different tone. Ibn Arabi sees this renewal of creational force in a Quranic verse, "Each day he is upon some task" (Q 55:29). God's "task" is the creation, he explains, and "day" is each invisible moment. Therefore in each instant God undertakes a new task and changes his relationship to every existent thing in the universe.[12]

God's creating act is interfused with the name All-merciful (*al-Rahman*). In his eternal existence, God the All-merciful speaks and his breath becomes articulated in each thing in the universe. A Quranic verse reads that "Our only word to a thing, when we desire it, is to say to it 'Be!,' so it comes to be." (Q 16:40); accordingly, for Ibn Arabi, when God speaks the one word 'Be!' it gives rise to the endless succession of words and worlds.[13] When he speaks, it is the mercy that issues

---

[11] Ibn al-Arabi, *The Bezels of Wisdom (Fusus al-Hikam)*, trans. R.W.J. Austin (New York: Paulist Press, 1980), 50.

[12] Chittick, *The Sufi Path of Knowledge*, 18.

[13] Chittick, *Ibn Arabi: Heir to the Prophets*, 58-59.

forth from him in the form of the breath which Ibn Arabi calls *al-nafas al-Rahmani*, breath of All-merciful. Therefore mercy is the ontological basis for creation and it brings into existence every individual essence.

> Every essence asks for existence from God. Accordingly God's mercy extends to, and covers, every essence. For God, by the very mercy that he exercises upon it, accepts the thing's latent desire to exist and brings it out to existence. This is why we assert that the mercy of God extends to everything both in actual reality and possibility.[14]

In order to understand the position of human being in this totality of the creation we need to turn back to *Fusus al-Hikam*. There Ibn Arabi explains that the creation of the cosmos does not satisfy God's desire to be mirrored because it lacks the spirit in it. "The Reality gave existence to the whole cosmos (at first) as an undifferentiated thing without anything of the spirit in it, so that it was like an unpolished mirror."[15] Adam as the archetype of humankind represents the polished mirror that has received the spirit and is equipped to reflect all the names of God. The human being is the finishing touch that ensures meaning for the whole universe. Ibn Arabi compares Adam (in relation to cosmos) to the pupil of the eye through which the act of seeing takes place; or to the seal in the ring which encloses and preserves a King's treasure.[16]

As has been said before, for Ibn Arabi human beings have the potential to reflect all the names of God in their being. This ability, however, remains a potential and requires work to reach the expected prospective. The ideal mirroring of God is accomplished through assuming the traits of the divine names (*takhalluq bi-akhlaq Allah*). The Arabic term *akhlaq* alludes both to the character traits engraved in a person from creation and also to the morals in accordance with which one should lead his/her life. Therefore through his choice of words, Ibn Arabi holds equal assuming the traits of God with reaching perfect ethics. There is an appropriate level of reflection for each name of God

---

[14] Toshihiko Izutsu, *Sufism and Taoism: A Comparative Study of Key Philosophical Concepts* (Berkeley: University of California Press, 1984), 118.
[15] *Bezels of Wisdom*, 50.
[16] Ibid., 51.

and for Ibn Arabi, the names that indicate God's mercy and love always surpass the names that designate his anger, power, and dominance. In accordance with God's mercy having precedence over other qualities of God, love and mercy should be reflected in human beings more than any other name of God.[17]

In the same vein with each created thing, each of God's prophets has the potency to reflect certain names of God better than others. Although each prophet represents a specific name in the perfect manner, none of the prophets is able to reflect God in all his inclusiveness. It is only the constitution of Prophet Muhammad that is able to manifest God in the all-comprehensive manner he deserves.

> ... each prophet possesses a specific and curtailed constitution while Muhammad possesses an all-inclusive one ... once you know this and once you desire to see the Real in the most perfect manner in which he can become manifest in this human plane, then you need to know that this does not belong to you. You do not have a constitution like that possessed by Muhammad. Whenever the Real discloses himself to you within the mirror of your heart, your mirror will make him manifest to you in the measure of its constitution and in the form of its shape. You know how far you stand below Muhammad's degree in knowledge of his Lord through his plane. So cling to faith and follow him! Place him before you as the mirror within which you gaze upon your own form and the form of others. When you do this, you will come to know that God must disclose himself to Muhammad within his mirror. I have already told you that the mirror displays an effect in that which is seen from the point of view of the observer who sees. So the manifestation of the Real within the mirror of Muhammad is the most perfect, most balanced, and most beautiful manifestation, because of mirror's actuality. When you perceive him in the mirror of Muhammad, you will have perceived from him a perfection which you could not perceive in respect of considering your own mirror.[18]

---

[17] Ibn Arabi, *The Sufi Path of Knowledge*, 22-23.
[18] Ibid., 352, from *Futuhat al-Makkiyya*, III, 251:3.

In this passage, Ibn Arabi's exhortation to the seeker of the divine manifestation is to place Muhammad before himself as the mirror within which he can gaze upon the perfect reflection of God. This is exactly the same advice Clare gives to Agnes regarding Jesus. Both Clare and Ibn Arabi believe that although each human being carries the mirror of the heart in their own being; the perfect mirroring of the divine, however, can only be actualized through special products – if you will – of creation. Furthermore Ibn Arabi develops a high theology around the spirit of Muhammad that is reminiscent of the logos in Christian tradition. The perfect character of Muhammad, which Ibn Arabi calls "the Muhammadan reality," is created from the light of God before the creation of the cosmos. This spirit of Muhammad – also identified with *al-insan al-kamil*, the complete human – is represented by other prophets in a limited form before the appearance of Muhammad in Mecca. The spirit also carries a cosmological importance as the *barzakh al-ala*, the highest mediation point between the corporeal and spiritual worlds. Without going into details of Ibn Arabi's complicated cosmology, suffice it to say that the idealization of Muhammad as the perfect human being goes beyond the classical Muslim understanding of Muhammad as solely a prophet. In surpassing this point of view, Ibn Arabi pictures the Muhammadan spirit in terms that are very close to the idea of logos in the Christian tradition.

On the other hand, the perfection of Muhammad is closely tied to God's mercy in Ibn Arabi's understanding, very much like the Christian association of Jesus with love. In the Quran, God calls upon Muhammad saying "we have sent you only as a mercy to the worlds" (Q 21:107). Since mercy always prevails over all of the other attributes of God, it is only plausible that mercy becomes manifested in Muhammad in accordance with the special place it has in the divinity. Thus Ibn Arabi sees mercy in the mirror of Muhammad, in the same way Clare sees humility and love in the mirror of Jesus. Ibn Arabi also identifies himself with the mercy as the last inheritor of the Muhammadan spirit. He writes, "God created me as a mercy, and he made me an heir to the mercy of him (Muhammad) to whom God said, 'we sent thee only as a mercy to the worlds.'"[19] In another instance, he records one

---

[19] Chittick, "Ibn Arabi's Hermeneutics of Mercy," in *Mysticism and Sacred Scripture*, ed. Steven T. Katz (Oxford: Oxford University Press, 2000), 156; from *Futuhat*, IV 163:9.

of his visions in which he saw himself in the ranks of the angels who held up the great columns of the throne upon which the All-merciful was sitting. He saw himself supporting the most excellent of them all which was "the store of mercy," because he believed that God created him "compassionate in an unqualified sense."[20]

Mirroring capacity of Muhammad in Ibn Arabi's understanding comes very close to that of Jesus in Clare's writings from these perspectives. These mystics identify the perfect mirror they aim to place within their hearts in accordance with the religious tradition in which they were brought up. Despite the different personas they prefer to choose as the mirror, the characteristics they see in these mirrors do not diverge. The poverty, humility and charity that Clare distinguishes in the mirror of Jesus correspond directly to the mercy Ibn Arabi sees in the mirror of Muhammad. Let us hope, therefore, that these two great mystics might teach us to see beyond the labels and titles that restrict our vision. The mirror of the heart that each of us possesses is able to do this, if we can only let it function freely in accordance with its divinely intended prospective.

---

[20] Ibid., 156, from *Futuhat* III, 431:32.

Ibn al-Farīḍ: Francis's Sufi Contemporary

Michael D. Calabria, O.F.M.

Introduction

There is an old saying in Arabic: *Maṣr umm id-dunya* – "Egypt (or Cairo) is the mother of the world." While certainly a hyperbole, it nevertheless highlights the significant role that Egypt has played in human history and culture. This is particularly true with regard to the Abrahamic faiths all of which took root and thrived on Egyptian soil. As it had done for Christianity, Egypt made significant contributions to Islamic theology and spirituality signified above all by Cairo's al-Azhar Mosque and University, one of the preeminent religious institutions in the Islamic world to this day. Egypt's capital is likewise home to numerous mausoleums, shrines, and cenotaphs of members of the Prophet Muhammad's family.[1] For Franciscans, Egypt's importance lies, of course, in that it was the scene of the encounter between Francis and the Ayyubid Sultan al-Malik al-Kamil in 1219.

While Egypt historically served as the power base of the Fatimid, Ayyubid and Mamluk empires, it has also been home to the *fuqarā'*, literally the "poor ones" – the holy men and women who shunned wealth, power and prestige, and directed their hearts, minds, and bodies to *dhikr* and *samā'*, the recollection of God and attentiveness to his Word, that they might experience *fanā* and *baqā*, the mystical annihilation of the self and abiding in God – the men and women we call *sufis*.

While the names of Persian mystics such as Rumi (1207-1273 / A.H. 605-672) and Hafez (d. 1391 / A.H. 793), or Andalusians like Ibn al-'Arabi (1165-1240 / A.H. 560-638) are most often evoked in discussions of Sufism, Egyptian Sufis are among some of the most significant

---

[1] Principal among them is the mosque and shrine of Hussein ibn 'Ali, the grandson of the Prophet who was martyred at the battle of Karbala in 680, and whose head was brought to Cairo in the twelfth century. See Galila El Kadi and Alain Bonnamy, *Architecture for the Dead: Cairo's Medieval Necropolis* (Cairo: AUC Press, 2007).

and revered of their tradition. Among them is Dhū'l-Nun al-Maṣri (c. 796-860 / A.H. 180-245), regarded as the "the father of Moslem theosophy";[2] the poet Busiri (1213-1296 / A.H. 610-695) who composed one of the most renowned and revered poems in the Muslim world, the "Poem of the Mantle" (al-Burdah); and Ibn 'Ata Allah al-Iskandari (d. 1309 / A.H. 709) who successfully defended Sufism from verbal attacks during the Mamluk era, and whose writings have enjoyed popularity throughout the Islamic world.

There is one Sufi, in particular however, that I believe merits the attention not only of Muslims but of Franciscans as well: Abu al-Qāsim'Umar ibn al-Shaykh Abu al-Hasan 'Ali ibn al-Murshid ibn 'Ali or, as he is far more commonly and simply known, 'Umar ibn al-Fāriḍ (1181-1235 / A.H. 576-632). He has been called the "the greatest Sufi poet of the Arabic language"[3] and "master of the Arabic mystical ode."[4] Within a century of his death, he was regarded as a saint (walī) whose burial place became a popular shrine that is visited by devotees to this day. Ibn al-Fāriḍ has particular interest for Franciscans due to the fact that this *faqīr* – this "poor man" of Egypt – is an exact contemporary of Francis, the "poor man of Assisi," having been born in the same year (1181), and surviving Francis by less than a decade. They are both therefore contemporaries of the sultan al-Mālik al-Kāmil (1180-1228) around whom their lives nearly converged. Additionally, their hagiographies bear striking similarities, as do their spiritualities. By examining the life and works of Ibn al-Fāriḍ, we gain a glimpse into the Muslim world that Francis entered in the summer of 1219, and perhaps come to a better understanding of why his encounter with the Sultan may have been a meeting of hearts and minds. Moreover, I believe we may gain a greater appreciation for the similar ways in which Muslims and Franciscans express notions of sanctity and holiness, and our love and quest for God.

---

[2] R.A. Nicholson, *The Mystics of Islam* (London: Arkana, 1989), 79.

[3] Seyyed Hossein Nasr, *The Garden of Truth* (New York: HarperOne, 2007), 188.

[4] John Renard, *Seven Doors to Islam* (Berkeley: University of California, 1996), 119.

Biography and Hagiography

With regard to Francis of Assisi, we are fortunate to have a number of documents that convey autobiographical or biographical information and help us to know his character relatively well in spite of the eight centuries that separate us. Beyond his own writings, there are a number of "lives" that, however hagiographical, can still be mined for biographical information. If nothing else, they reveal to us the way Francis was regarded in the decades after his death.[5]

We are somewhat more impoverished when it comes to sources for Ibn al-Fāriḍ. The entire corpus of his writings that can be authentically attributed to him essentially consists of fifteen poems or odes (*qaṣīdah/qaṣā'id*), the most celebrated of which are the lengthy "Poem of the (Sufi) Way" (*Naẓm al-Sulūk*, also called *al-Tā'īyah al-Kubrā*, the "the Greater Poem Rhyming in T"), and the "Wine Ode" (*al-Khamrīyah*), as well as a number of quatrains and riddles. These were collected and published ca. 1333, almost a century after the poet's death, by his grandson 'Alī Sibṭ Ibn al-Fāriḍ (the son of an unnamed daughter of Ibn al-Fāriḍ) who was born sometime after 1235. 'Alī prefaced his grandfather's *Dīwān* (collected poems) with a lengthy hagiographical proem (*dībājah*), undoubtedly undertaken to defend Ibn al-Fāriḍ's memory against charges of heresy by detailing his pious character and miracles.[6] 'Alī's proem includes alleged reminiscences of his uncle, Kamāl al-Dīn Muḥammad (d. 1290 / A.H. 689), Ibn al-Fāriḍ's son, who in turn claimed to be quoting his illustrious father.

Sources written by Ibn al-Fāriḍ's students, acquaintances, contemporaries or near contemporaries are few and rather limited in the biographical information they provide. Later Mamluk sources include polemics and subsequent defenses of the poet's orthodoxy, but add little to his biography.[7] The earliest biographical information we have

---

[5] These include the accounts written by Thomas of Celano, Julian of Speyer, Henri d'Avranches, and St. Bonaventure among others.

[6] The Arabic text has been published as Giuseppe Scattolin, *The Dīwān of Ibn al-Fāriḍ: Readings of its Text Throughout History* (Cairo: Institut Français d'Archéologie Orientale, 2004). The "Wine Ode," "Poem of the Sufi Way" and the Proem have been translated and published in: *'Umar Ibn al-Farid: Sufi Verse, Saintly Life*, Th. Emil Homerin, trans. (New York: Paulist Press, 2001).

[7] For a complete list of biographical sources for Ibn al-Fāriḍ, see Giuseppe Scattolin, "More on Ibn al-Fāriḍ's Biography," *MIDEO* 22 (1994): 197-242.

concerning Ibn al-Fāriḍ is an obituary notice from 1235 written by his student Zakī al-Dīn al-Mundhirī (1185-1258 / A.H. 581-656) who had become a *hadith* scholar and Sufi master in his own right, and who (coincidentally) served as head of the *madrasa* of al-Malik al-Kamil in Cairo for over twenty years.[8]

Al-Mundhirī provides us with Ibn al-Fāriḍ's basic biography: that he was born in March 1181, died in January 1235, and was buried the next day in the Qarāfah cemetery at the foot of Mount Muqattam on the south eastern edge of Cairo. Although his family was from the Syrian city of Hama, he himself was born and raised in Egypt. He belonged to the Shafi'ite school of law (favored by the Ayyubids), and studied *hadith*. Furthermore, al-Mundhirī remarks: "He spoke excellent poetry in accordance with the way of Sufism ['ala ṭariqāt al-taṣawwuf] ... In his poetry, he would combine purity of expression with sweetness."[9] Al-Mundhirī would later explain that the name "Ibn al-Fāriḍ" signifies that the poet was the son (*ibn*) of a women's advocate (*al-fāriḍ*). In addition, he mellifluously described his teacher as being:

> of gentle nature, a sweet pool and spring, of pure expression, refined of allusion, fluent and sublime in pronunciation and quotation. He pushed to the limits and then studied Sufism. So he became a variegated meadow, perfumed by beauty, clad with good nature, gathering from the generosity of the self all varieties [of good things].[10]

Al-Mundhirī mentions one of Ibn al-Fāriḍ's sons, but we know from later sources that he fathered two sons and a daughter. (We have no information whatsoever about his wife). Finally, we learn that Ibn al-Fāriḍ lived in Mecca for an unspecified amount of time, and after returning to Egypt, he took up residence in the mosque of al-Azhar in Cairo.[11]

---

[8] Scattolin, (1994), 231, n.7.

[9] Th. Emil Homerin, *From Arab Poet to Muslim Saint: Ibn al-Fāriḍ, His Verse, and His Shrine* (Cairo: American University in Cairo, 2001), 15. Homerin's book remains the most comprehensive overview of the poet in English.

[10] Homerin, *Arab Poet*, 16.

[11] Homerin, *Arab Poet*, 16.

The next significant source of biographical information comes from the Kurdish Muslim scholar Abu-l 'Abbas Ahmad ibn Khallikān (1211-82 / A.H. 608-680) who included information about Ibn al-Fāriḍ in his biographical dictionary *Wafayāt al-'āyān* ("The Obituaries of Eminent Men") completed in 1274, just thirty-nine years after the poet's death. Ibn Khallikān never mentions having met the poet, and clearly indicates he depended upon word of mouth for information about the poet's character: "I have heard that he was a pious, virtuous, and abstemious man."[12] He had a firsthand acquaintance with the poet's work, however, which he describes as "a charming fine collection of poetry in which his style is pure and elegant, and follows the manner of the way of the *fuqarā*' (lit., "the poor ones" – i.e. the Sufis), and actually quotes some of the poet's verses.[13]

The *Dībājah*

Similarities in the stories of Ibn al-Fāriḍ and Francis become apparent when we turn to the most extensive bio-/hagiographical source, the *Dībājah*, written by Ibn al-Fāriḍ's grandson 'Ali, which served as an introduction to his grandfather's *Dīwān*. Since, as noted above, 'Ali intended his proem to serve as a defense of his grandfather's orthodoxy it bears many of the same characteristics found in other Muslim hagiographies.[14] While we have no Cimabue-like portrait of Ibn al-Fāriḍ, 'Ali does provide a description of the poet comparable to that of Francis in

---

[12] Homerin, *Arab Poet*, 18.

[13] Sufis earned the designation as "poor ones" not only on account of their itinerant lifestyles but due to their emphasis on spiritual poverty. For Sufis, as well as for Franciscans, poverty signifies the realization that "all reality and all positive qualities belong to God and that in our basic nature we are the poor whereas He is the Rich." (Seyyed Hossein Nasr, 122). Sufis refer to passages from the Qur'an such as: "O people, you are the poor ones in relation to Allah, and God is the Rich One, the One who is Praised" (*al*-Fāṭir, 35.15). Thus, the Sufi is the "poor one" who is totally dependent upon Allah, and desires nothing but Allah. For an anthology of Sufi sayings about this subject, cf. Java Nurbakhsh, *Spiritual Poverty in Sufism* (London: Khaniqahi-Nimatullahi Publications, 1984).

[14] Cf. John Renard, *Friends of God: Islamic Images of Piety, Commitment, and Servanthood* (Berkeley: University of California, 2008).

Thomas of Celano's *First Life* (1C 83),[15] ostensibly quoting his uncle, Kamāl al-Dīn Muhammad, Ibn al-Fāriḍ's son:

> The shaykh – may God be satisfied with him – was of medium build, his face being handsome with a ruddy appearance. When he participated in an audition and went into ecstasy as a mystical state coming over him, his face would increase in beauty and brightness, and sweat would pour from the rest of him until it flowed beneath his feet onto the ground. [I have not seen among the Arabs or non-Arabs one as handsome of form, and I, of all people, resemble him the most in appearance ...] Further, when he walked in the city, people would crowd around him seeking spiritual blessings and benedictions, while trying to kiss his hand. But he would not allow anyone to do that; rather he shook hands with them. His clothes were fine and his odor fragrant. He would spend amply on those who visited him, being very generous.[16]

While we lack a *Testament* for Ibn al-Fāriḍ such as that written by Francis, ʿAli cites what he claims to be is his grandfather's own account of the beginning of his spiritual quest:

> When I began my detachment [from the world], I would ask my father's permission, and then go up to the *Wadi al-Mustaḍʾafīn* (lit.: "Valley of the Wretches") on the second mountain of Cairo's al-Muqattam where I stayed, wandering around night and day."[17]

While it is impossible to determine if these are actually Ibn al-Fāriḍ's own words, one is tempted to compare them to the beginning of Francis's *Testament*:

---

[15] *Francis of Assisi: Early Documents*, ed. Regis Armstrong, J.A. Wayne Hellmann, William Short, Vol. 1 *The Saint* (New York: New City Press, 1999), 252-53. Hereafter referred to *FA:ED* followed by volume and page.

[16] Homerin (*Ibn al-Fāriḍ*), 303-04.

[17] Ibid., 304. While citing Homerin's translation, I occasionally depart from it as in the case of the word *tajrīd* which I translate as "detachment" (vs. Homerin's "spiritual retreat"). It literally means "peeling or stripping off," a potent concept for Sufis in general, but as we shall see, particularly associated with Ibn al-Fāriḍ.

The Lord gave me, Brother Francis, thus to begin doing penance in this way: for when I was in sin, it seemed too bitter for me to see lepers. And the Lord himself led me among them and I showed mercy to them.[18]

In both accounts, Ibn al-Fāriḍ and Francis, like other Muslim and Christian holy men and women before them, marked the beginning of their spiritual journey of conversion by physically detaching themselves from their comfortable every day surroundings. Francis went among the lepers, while Ibn al-Fāriḍ (ostensibly) spoke of wandering in the "Valley of the Wretches" (*wādī al-mustaḍ'afīn*) located among the Muqattam hills on Cairo's southeastern fringe. While it has been suggested this valley referred to "a place of retreat for Sufis,"[19] the word *mustaḍ'afīn* more aptly refers to the poor and destitute, perhaps even including lepers, living on the fringes of Cairo. Whenever the word *mustaḍ'afūn/īn* is used in the Quran, it always refers to people who are weak, vulnerable and oppressed.[20] To this day parts of Muqattam continue to be associated with the poor and destitute as demonstrated by the village of garbage pickers (*zabbalīn*) that formed around Cairo's trash dump at the foot of these mountains at the end of the last century.[21]

Somewhat ironically, local tradition also associates the Muqattam hills with several of the prophets:

> According to these traditions, Noah's descendants settled here before founding the first major Egyptian city, Memphis. Jacob dwelt here at one time, and Joseph was initially buried beneath the Muqattam cliffs.... Even Jesus lent an aura of sanctity to the city by telling Mary that Muhammad's followers would eventually be buried below the Muqattam hills. One medieval

---

[18] *FA:ED* 1, 124.

[19] Giuseppe Scattolin suggests it was "probably a place of retreat for Sufis" ("More on Ibn al-Farid's Biography," *MIDEO* 22 (1994), 223.

[20] Quran 4.75, 98 and 127; 8.26. Muhammad Qasim Zamam, "Oppressed on Earth, The" in *Encyclopedia of the Qur'an* (Leiden: Brill, 2003), 580-83.

[21] Elena Volpi and Doaa Abdel Motaal, *The Zabbalin Community of Muqattam*, Cairo Papers in Social Science 19, no. 4 (Cairo: American University in Cairo, 1997).

legend holds that God gave the Muqattam hills their sacred status.[22]

According to Ali's proem, after periods of wandering, Ibn al-Fāriḍ would obediently return to his father, himself a man of great religious knowledge and assistant to the governor of Cairo, and sit with him in court and teaching sessions, until the desire for detachment would once again lead Ibn al-Fāriḍ away into the Muqattam hills. Wandering in the barren rocky terrain outside Cairo, Ibn al-Fāriḍ was in a sense imitating the prophet Muhammad (pbuh) who used to wander in the hills outside Mecca in the period before the first revelation of the Quran in a cave on Mount Ḥīrah. Thomas of Celano likewise relates how Francis, before he left the world, would go to a remote place with a companion, and then prayed alone in cave (IC 6).

Although, like Francis, Ibn al-Fāriḍ had little interest in his father's work, ʿAli's account makes no reference to any contention between Ibn al-Fāriḍ and his father such as in Francis's case. Rather, his father seems to have a deeply spiritual man himself who declined promotion to chief judge, eventually retired from public life, and devoted himself to the spiritual life at al-Azhar until his death. Then, says Ibn al-Fāriḍ, "I returned to detachment and wandering, following the path of Truth, but nothing was revealed to me."

The turning point in Ibn al-Fāriḍ's spiritual journey occurred when, having returned to his studies of Islamic law, he met an old green grocer (*baqqāl*), whom in typically youthful fashion, he upbraided for incorrectly performing the ablutions for prayers. Looking up at the self-righteous young man, the *baqqāl* addressed him by name, and told him that he would not receive enlightenment in Egypt [lit. "It will not be opened/revealed to you."], but only in Mecca: "So head for it, for the time of your enlightenment is near!" Ibn al-Fāriḍ thus recognized him as one of the "friends of God," a saint (*walī*), and assumed a more humble position at the feet of his master. When he expressed to his newfound teacher his inability to find transportation to Mecca outside the pilgrimage season, a vision of Mecca appeared before him and remained in his view until at last he arrived at the city where enlightenment came upon him.

---

[22] Renard, *Friends*, 202.

Somewhat similarly, Thomas of Celano (1C 17) recounts a story in which the young Francis encountered someone beneath his station, a beggar seeking alms, whom Francis likewise rebuked. Although the beggar did not reveal himself as a spiritual guide, the incident had such an impact on Francis, that according to Celano, Francis "was immediately led to penance."

In Islamic hagiography, the extraordinary ability to communicate with animals is characteristic of God's prophets including Solomon, Jesus, and Muhammad, as well as many saints including Ibn al-Fāriḍ.[23] According to 'Ali, when Ibn al-Fāriḍ was in the Hijāz, he stayed in an oasis that was a ten day's ride from Mecca. Miraculously, however, he was able to make a daily journey to Mecca to pray at the Ka'aba. In order to expedite the trip, a large lion approached the shaykh and offered to take him to Mecca upon his back, but the shaykh refused, and so the lion simply accompanied him on the daily journey.[24] In addition to this tale, we are told that Ibn al-Fāriḍ "used to be on friendly terms with wild animals night and day."[25] Among Christian saints, Francis, above all, seems to have possessed this ability to communicate with animals. Thomas of Celano writes of Francis preaching to birds who listened attentively, and exhorting "all animals, all reptiles, and also insensible creatures, to praise and love the Creator" (1C 58). For Celano, Francis's ability to communicate with all creatures was an indication that he had "already passed into the freedom of the glory of the children of God" (1C 81).

According to 'Ali, Ibn al-Fāriḍ stayed in Mecca for fifteen years, although the early accounts of al-Mundhirī and Ibn Khallikān do not specify the length of his sojourn there. We are likewise told that Ibn al-Fāriḍ met the Baghdadi Sufi Shihāb al-Dīn al-Suhrawardī in Mecca in the year 1231 (A.H. 638). Since the biographical accounts generally agree that Ibn al-Fāriḍ died in Cairo in 1235 at age 54, we might therefore conclude that he departed for Mecca in 1216 at age thirty-five, and remained there until at least 1231 when he returned to Egypt just four years before his death. This would place him outside of Egypt during the Fifth Crusade (1217-1221).

---

[23] Renard, *Friends*, 3, 24, 33, 58, 271.

[24] This tale is evocative of Muhammad's (pbuh) night journey ('isrā') to Mecca on the back of Burāq.

[25] Homerin, *Ibn al-Fāriḍ*, 306.

Others, however, have expressed skepticism about the "round number" of fifteen years, and are inclined to think that the poet remained in Mecca for perhaps as little as two or three years, having started out in his mid-20s rather than his mid-30s, and then returning to Mecca for a second visit in 1231 at which time he met al-Suhrawardī.[26] While Th. Emil Homerin, a leading translator of Ibn al-Fāriḍ's works, does not completely dismiss the possibility of a fifteen-year sojourn, he has demonstrated, however, that Ibn al-Fāriḍ must been back in Cairo *before* 1223 since a student completed *hadith* studies with him that year. Without additional corroborating texts, it is thus impossible to fix a chronology for Ibn al-Fāriḍ's life, and therefore impossible to determine if Ibn al-Fāriḍ was in Egypt during Francis's visit in 1219. Even if Ibn al-Fāriḍ were in Egypt at this time, he would not have had the opportunity to meet the Poor Man of Assisi since the poet seems to have resided at al-Azhar in Cairo for the remainder of his life while Francis's stay in Egypt seems to have been limited to the area around Damietta and the Sultan's camp at Fariskur. As we shall see, however, their paths nearly converged around al-Mālik al-Kāmil.

'Ali tells us that Ibn al-Fāriḍ's return to Cairo was prompted when he miraculously heard the voice of the *baqqāl*, his spiritual guide, who was on his death bed in Egypt. When he arrived at his master's side, the *baqqāl* conjured up yet another vision, this time of the plot of land where he wished to be buried. According to 'Ali, this plot was precisely where his grandfather was later buried, that is, at the foot of Mount Muqattam, and probably not too far from the "Valley of the Wretches" where Ibn al-Fāriḍ used to wander as a young man.

For the remainder of his life, Ibn al-Fāriḍ resided at al-Azhar, where he composed poetry, and gathered around him a group of students and devotees which, according to 'Ali's proem, included "respected jurisprudents, mendicants, and judges, and great men of state, including amirs, viziers, and the leaders of the people."[27] Among those who learned of the Shaykh's prodigious poetic talents was the sultan al-Mālik al-Kāmil. 'Ali wrote in his proem that the Sultan "loved scholars, and he would meet with them in a special session for them alone."

---

[26] A.J. Arberry, *The Mystical Poems of Ibn al-Farid* (Dublin: Emery Walker, 1956), 9-10.

[27] Homerin, *Ibn al-Fāriḍ*, 303.

Ibn Khallikān echoes ʿAli's remarks[28] as does the eminent Egyptian historian al-Maqrīzi (1364-1442), adding that the Sultan:

> [G]ave lodging with him in the Citadel to several men of learning.... Beds were set up for them beside his so that they might lie on them and converse through the night. Learning and literature flourished under him, and men of distinction resorted to his court. To those who came to him he provided a full and generous living.[29]

On one such evening, the Sultan challenged his learned guests to recite a poem with as many verses as possible ending with the sound "ai" (i.e. the letter *yā'* preceded by the *fatHa*), this being among the rarest and most difficult of rhymes in Arabic. While the Sultan outdid most of his learned guests, his secretary, Sharaf al-Dīn, recited still a longer poem with this rhyming scheme. The poem recalled the passionate but onerous desire of a man to be reunited with a maiden he had fallen in love with in the Hijāz – the mystical poet's most common metaphor of the spiritual quest: "Ah, how I yearn for her radiant face, and how my heart thirsts for those dear red lips!"[30]

Moved by the poet's ardent verses, the Sultan demanded to know the name and whereabouts of the poet. When Sharaf al-Dīn told him of the shaykh who resided at al-Azhar, the Sultan commanded him:

> Take one thousand of our dinars and go to him and say on my behalf, 'Your son Muhammad [al-Malik al-Kamil] greets you and requests that you accept this from him in the name of the mendicants (*al-fuqarā'*) who come to you.' If he accepts this sum, ask him to present himself to me that we may profit from his blessings.[31]

---

[28] *Wafayāt al-ʿāyān* (Beirut: Dar Assakafa, n.d.), vol. 5, 81.

[29] *A History of the Ayyūbid Sultans of Egypt*, R.J.C. Broadhurst, trans. (Boston: Twayne, 1980), 229, 231.

[30] *Dīwān*, 1.51; Arberry, 13.51. For references to the *Dībājah* and odes, I provide references to the Arabic text in the *Dīwān* (Scattolin edition, 2004), and the English translation done by Arberry.

[31] Homerin, *Ibn al-Fāriḍ*, 321.

Knowing the Shaykh's reputation for asceticism and afraid of insulting the holy man, the secretary pleaded not to be sent on such a mission: "for he will not accept gold, nor will he come with me to attend you." The Sultan insisted, however, and as predicted, when Sharaf al-Dīn approached Ibn al-Fāriḍ, he was soundly rebuffed and rebuked, and forbidden to return to the Shaykh for a year. Struck by both the poet's refusal of his offer, and by his secretary's distress at not being able to see the shaykh for a year, al-Kāmil decided to make a surprise visit to the poet setting out in disguise and under the cover of night. The Shaykh eluded him, however, and fled to Alexandria. When Ibn al-Fāriḍ finally returned to Cairo, the indefatigable Sultan sent word requesting the Shaykh's permission to build a tomb for him in the mausoleum of Imam al-Shafi'ī, next to the grave of the Sultan's own mother. When the Shaykh rejected this, the Sultan offered to build him a tomb that would serve as a shrine. This, too, was rejected. Undoubtedly, Ibn al-Fāriḍ refused such royal patronage as he did not wish to be considered a propagandist court poet such as Ibn 'Unayn (1154-1233 / A.H. 549-630) who was part of the Sultan's "Ministry of Composition" (*Dīwān al-Inshā'*).[32] It appears, therefore, that the Sultan never met one of the most famous holy men of his realm, and yet ironically did receive the holy man of another realm and religion.

The Sultan's offer of gifts and honors, and Ibn al-Fāriḍ's subsequent refusal finds a parallel in Celano's account of the Sultan's meeting with Francis:

> The Sultan honored him as much as he could, offering him many gifts, trying to turn his mind to worldly riches. But when he saw that he resolutely scorned all these things like dung, the Sultan was overflowing with admiration and recognized him as man unlike any other. (1C 57)

While some have seen this story of the Sultan and Ibn al-Fāriḍ as a part of 'Ali's attempt to rehabilitate his grandfather's reputation,[33] the story is consistent with the Sultan's love for men of wisdom and learn-

---

[32] Homerin, *Arab Poet*, 103, n. 20. Cf. al-Maqrizi, *History*, 188f.
[33] E.g. Issa Boulatta, "Toward a Biography of Ibn al-Farid," *Arabica* 28 (1981): 48.

ing. It is also consistent with Ayyubid patronage of Sufis.[34] The Sultan's apparent fascination with Francis could very well have been due to his resemblance to the *fuqarā'* – the poor ones, the Sufis – in his appearance, manner and speech. Although the Sultan was certainly familiar with Coptic monks, Francis's Order of poor, itinerant "lesser brothers" would have seemed to him more like a Sufi brotherhood (*ṭarīqah*).

One of the best known episodes in the life of Francis is his stripping naked before the bishop, a gesture by which he dramatically rejected his father's wealth and claim on him (1C 15). Poignantly, at the end of his life, he asked his brothers to lay him naked on the ground, emulating Christ naked on the Cross (2C 217). Similarly, Ibn al-Fāriḍ also acquired a reputation for stripping off his clothes according to 'Ali, albeit for different reasons. He records a story told by the poet's son in which Ibn al-Fāriḍ was strolling through a Cairo market when he heard a group of guards singing:

> Master, we stayed awake all night seeking union with you.
> But you didn't allow it, master, so we dreamed of your phantom form.
>
> But master, even that didn't come,
> So there is no doubt that we're not on your mind!

Upon hearing this, Ibn al-Fāriḍ started screaming and dancing. As a crowd gathered around him, he began to strip off (ظ) his clothing as did they. Clad only in his undergarments, the poet was carried off to al-Azhar where he remained for some days in something like a trance.[35] This motif of stripping occurs in Ibn al-Fāriḍ's odes as a metaphor for removing all that prevents someone from loving God completely:

> I have stripped myself of shame, and discarded the acceptance
> of my piety and my accepted pilgrimages …

---

[34] Salah al-Dīn, al-Kāmil's uncle, built a residence in Cairo for Sufi brotherhoods which housed three hundred Sufis. See Michael Chamberlain, "The Crusader Era and the Ayyubid Dynasty," *The Cambridge History of Egypt*, volume 1 (Cambridge: Cambridge University Press, 1998), 231; André Raymond, *Cairo* (New York: Rizzoli Universe Promotional Books, 2003), 94-95.

[35] Homerin, *Ibn al-Fāriḍ*, 319.

Good news for you, so strip yourself of all that is upon you for you have been remembered even though what is within you is crooked ...

Hold fast to the hem of passion's skirts, and strip yourself of shame
And abandon the path of the pious ones, revered though they may be.[36]

In a similar fashion, in the "Poem of the Sufi Way," he writes of how some people are ashamed of his "nakedness:"

Stripping off modesty is my duty to you even though
My people refuse to come near me (as) impropriety is my habit.

But they are not my people as long as they find fault with my exposure,
Showing their hatred, seeing fit to rough me up for your sake.

But my people are in the religion of love, the people
Who approved of my nakedness and found joy in my exposure.[37]

Spirituality: "The Prince of Lovers"

Even though his opus is relatively modest when compared to other Sufi poets and authors, explicating the essence of Ibn al-Fāriḍ's theology and spirituality presents a great challenge due to the difficulty of the poetical language he employs as well as the esoteric nature of his thought. I will attempt here to briefly describe some of the principal characteristics of his spirituality, particularly those that find resonance in the Franciscan tradition. In the world of Arabic literature, Ibn al-Fāriḍ is known as the "Prince of lovers" (*sultān al-'āshiqīn*) due to the motif he most commonly employs in his poetry, that of the lover who experiences the pain of separation (*al-farq*) from his beloved and a yearning for reunion (*al-ittiHād*), a metaphor for his desire to experi-

---

[36] *Dīwān*, 10.24, 44; 15.7; Arberry, 2.24, 44; 9.7
[37] *Dīwān* 4.78-80; Homerin, *Ibn al-Fāriḍ*, "Poem of the Sufi Way," vv.78-80.

ence a universal, all-comprehensive union (*al-jam'a*) with the Divine.[38] As such, he has much in common with other medieval Sufis, such as Hāfiz, as well as the Franciscan mystic Angela of Foligno (1248-1309), and other Christian mystics such as Gertrude of Helfta (1256-1302) and John of the Cross (1542-91). The Beloved of Ibn al-Fāriḍ's poems may be referred to as either male or female, and in either case, passionate, erotic imagery is often used as in the "bridal mysticism" of the medieval Christian tradition. The sober bitterness of separation from the Beloved is contrasted with the intoxicating sweetness of reunion. The separation is vividly described in terms of sickness, wasting away, and sleeplessness. This excerpt from one of Ibn al-Fāriḍ's poems exhibits several of these elements:

> Eyelids, sleepless for You, longing for You!
> And a heart in ardent desire, cleaved!
>
> And ribs wasted, nearly straightened by the passion,
> The terrible pain from deep within.
>
> And tears flowed; if not for panting breaths of hot air
> I would not have escaped the relentlessness.
>
> And how good are the illnesses (suffered) for you
> By which I am hidden from myself…
>
> I came to you in the morning as I did in the evening, downcast,
> And yet I did not say anxiously: "O my problems, leave me!"
>
> I hurry to every heart occupied with passion,
> And to every tongue devoted to love,
>
> And to every ear deaf to insult,
> And to every eyelid that has not given in to slumber.
>
> There was no love where tear-ducts were dry,
> And no passion where desire did not burn.
>
> Torment me as You will, except for being far from You.

---

[38] Scattolin prefers the designation: "Poet of the universal and all-comprehensive union, because this is the highest purpose and fullest realization of his mystical quest" (*Dīwān*, 7).

You will find me the most faithful lover, delighted in whatever pleases You.

And take the remainder of what you have left of my life
For there is no good in love that spares the heart ...³⁹

Weeping incessant tears, often flecked with blood as the lover mourns the absence of the Beloved, is a common theme in Ibn al-Fāriḍ's poetry:

Look upon a heart that is melted with ardent love for you,
And an eye overwhelmed in the waves of its blood-flecked tears.⁴⁰

Similarly, according to several Franciscan sources, Francis was given to intense bouts of crying as he recalled Christ's Passion. As Bonaventure wrote:

[H]e taught those who strive after the perfect life to cleanse themselves daily with streams of tears. Although he had already attained extraordinary purity of heart and body,] he did not cease to cleanse the eyes of his soul with a continuous flood of tears, unconcerned about the loss of his bodily sight.... He preferred to lose his sight rather than to repress the devotion of his spirit and hold back the tears which cleansed his interior vision so that he could see God.⁴¹

Although the Lover of Ibn al-Fāriḍ's poems frequently laments the separation from the Beloved, he is comforted by the signs of his Beloved in the sensory world in a way that is reminiscent of Francis's *Canticle of the Creatures*:

---

³⁹ *Dīwān* 10.3-12; Arberry, 2.3-12.
⁴⁰ *Dīwān* 10.40; Arberry, 2.40.
⁴¹ Bonaventure, *Major Legend of St. Francis*, 8; Cf. *The Legend of the Three Companions*, 14 and *The Remembrance of the Desire of a Soul*, 11; *FA:ED* 2, 5:8, 565-66; 5:14, 76; VI:11, 250. Of course, in Francis's case, at least some of this "weeping" may have actually been a symptom of eye disease (ophthalmia or trachoma) which the sources also describe.

Though he is absent from me, every sense sees him,
In every lovely, pure and beautiful expression.

In the melody of the lyre and gentle flute
When they embrace in trilling notes of song,

And in the verdant meadows of gazelles
In twilight's cool and daybreak's glow,

And in the dew of the clouds
on a blossoming carpet woven from flowers,

And in breezes, the wisps of wind,
when guiding the sweetest balm to me at dawn,

And in kissing the mouth of the cup,
sipping drops of wine in pure pleasure.

I never knew exile while he was with me,
And wherever we were together my mind was untroubled.[42]

With a length of 761 verses, Ibn al-Fāriḍ's "Poem of the Sufi Way" is considered the fullest and most mature expression of his thought, and is indeed the longest poem of its kind in Arabic. In it we move from ecstatic intoxication to enlightened sobriety.[43] As we have already seen in his shorter poems, the besotted Lover begins by detailing the pain and suffering he has endured for the Beloved. She chastises him, however, explaining that he has still not given himself to her completely and that he must sacrifice his very self:

For you never loved so long as you were not lost in me,
and you will never be lost without my form in you revealed
(vs.99).

This he accomplishes by transcending intoxicating passion with a sober effacement of his will and desire: "So I became a beloved, indeed one loving himself" (vs.205) and "I was none other than her" (vs.212). Drawing upon images of the rites of the *hajj*, he describes his journey to his self such that his heart is the Ka'aba of Mecca; his *Tawāf*

---

[42] *Dīwān*, 10.29-35. My translation is based on Homerin's (15).
[43] Homerin, *Ibn al-Fāriḍ*, 68.

– circling around the Ka'aba "is really circling around me;" and in his *sa'ee* – the ritual running between the hills of Safa and Marwah – "I run toward myself" (vs.450). The *Isrā'* – the night journey of Muhammad (pbuh) – becomes the "night journey of my inner heart" (vs.454). He, like Muhammad (pbuh), becomes a *rasūl* – a messenger: "I was a messenger sent to me, from me, and by my signs, my being was led to me" (vs.460). Only then does he realize that the Holy Spirit (*rūH al-qudus*) that he sought without was actually within: "I sought her from myself, she was there all along; how strange that I concealed her from me" (vs.412). In words echoed later in St. Bonaventure's *Itinerarium*,[44] it is in the mirror of the self that he finds himself: "I was gazing into the mirror of my beauty to see the perfection of my being in my contemplation of my face" (vs.517). The seeker is likewise exhorted to "contemplate what you see clearly without question in the polished mirrors, if you seek to uncover your self" (v.660). As a witness of the abiding oneness (*baqā 'aHadiyyatī*), the poet now sees the truth underlying all religions:

> So if the prayer niche of a mosque is illuminated by the Revelation [of the Qur'an]
> Then a church's altar is not worthless [i.e. is rendered useful] because of the Gospel,
>
> And the scriptures of the Torah of Moses [came] to his people,
> So that the rabbis might refer to it every night.
>
> And if a devotee prostrates before the stone [idols] in a temple
> Do not vow intolerance with fanaticism
>
> For surely many of those who are free from the shame of pagan idolatry
> Worship the *dinar*.
>
> And surely my revelation has reached those who heed
> And by me the revelation has arisen among every people.
>
> The vision of every faith has never strayed,

---

[44] Bonaventure, *Itinerarium Mentis in Deum*, ed. Philotheus Boehner and Zachary Hayes (St. Bonaventure, NY: Franciscan Institute Publications, 2002), Chapter 3, 81.

Nor have the thoughts of any creed.

One dazed in desire for the sun is not deranged,
For it shines from the light of my unveiled dazzling splendor
(vv. 733-39).

THE DEATH OF A SAINT

The biographical sources agree that Ibn al-Fāriḍ passed away at al-Azhar on the second of Jumada al-Awwal, 632 AH (January 1235) and was buried at the foot of Mt. Muqattam where the young poet used to wander and where the *baqqāl* had been buried. 'Ali wrote that his grandfather died following an ecstatic state such as that described above which precipitated the "stripping incident." He follows this rather succinct report of his grandfather's death with a much longer and fantastic tale that involves the Sufi poet and preacher Ibrahim al-Ja'barī (1202-88 / A.H. 599-687). Wandering in meditation near the Euphrates, al-Ja'barī was visited by a mysterious stranger who recited for him a verse of Ibn al-Fāriḍ's "Poem of the Sufi Way." Having identified the poet for al-Ja'barī, the stranger told him of the poet's imminent death in Cairo, and then led him to the side of the dying shaykh. Ibn al-Fāriḍ recognized al-Ja'barī as one of the "chosen friends of God" (*awliyā*), and asked him to attend his death, prepare his body for burial and stay at his grave for three days. Al-Ja'barī describes an "awesome funeral procession" with people crowding around the bier and green and white birds hovering over it."[45] Thomas of Celano likewise describes the unusual presence and behavior of birds on the eve of Francis's death, noting that larks, which usually avoid darkness, circled nosily over the house where Francis lay dying: "Whether they were showing their joy or their sadness with their song, we do not know."[46]

Although over the centuries dogmatic theologians have challenged Ibn al-Fāriḍ's orthodoxy, accusing him of propagating mystical union (*ittiHād*), monism (*waHdat al-wujūd*) and incarnationism (*Hulūl*), popular veneration of the saint has rarely wavered. By the fourteenth centu-

---

[45] According to 'Ali's proem, green and white birds had also attended the funeral of the *baqqāl*. Their presence apparently signifies that the deceased was a "martyr of love."

[46] *The Treatise on the Miracles of Saint Francis* 32, in *FA:ED* 2, 415.

ry Ibn al-Fāriḍ's grave had become a popular site for pilgrimage maintained by endowments from Mamluk rulers who paid for the upkeep of the tomb, the celebration of the saint's *mawlid* (festival day), and provided alms for the mendicants who gathered there.[47] In time, the tomb-complex came to include a congregational mosque and a soup kitchen for mendicants. Visiting Egypt in 1670, the Ottoman author and traveler Evilya Čelebī noted that five- to six-thousand people of all social classes crowded into mosque and shrine every Friday to recite from the Quran, pray and perform *dhikr*:

> All the people sit on one another's knees. Elite and commoners do not find each other disagreeable but all participate together with common purpose. It is a marvel! This kind of spiritual unity is not to be found at other shrines.[48]

Conclusion

I first read Th. Emil Homerin's study of Ibn al-Fāriḍ *From Arab Poet to Muslim Saint* in 2001 when I was living in Egypt. The similarities in the poet's biography, hagiography and spirituality to those of Francis quickly became apparent. Although from different faiths and cultures, these two medieval men, from the East and the West, felt the call of the Spirit, a call that would cause them to renounce the status, prestige and material wealth that their fathers had earned for them, in exchange for the life of a pilgrim and disciple, who embarked on a spiritual journey that first led them among the *mustaḍ'afīn*, the *minores*, the wretched and oppressed of the world. They both came to recognize the need to lighten their load on this journey by stripping away exterior and interior hindrances, and both came to see signs, reflections, and vestiges of God in the world around them, in others, and in themselves. Both seem to have had an experience of the Divine Presence in ways that precious few have or ever will. Yet, those of us who read their words, reflect on their lives, and follow their example somehow have an experience of God precisely because of these two individuals.

---

[47] Th. Emil Homerin, "The Domed Shrine of Ibn al-Fariḍ," *Annales Islamologiques* XXV (1991): 134.
[48] Homerin, *Arab Poet*, 78.

Poignantly for me, as a Franciscan friar living in Cairo, the lives of these two holy men virtually converged in Egypt, around the figure of the Sultan al-Malik al-Kamil. Upon my return to United States, I began to study Homerin's translation of the *Wine Ode* and the *Poem of the Sufi Way*, and more recently his other poems (*qaṣā'id*) in Arabic. It was then that I came to appreciate the exceptional beauty and profundity of the shaykh's words, what I might glean for my own spiritual life, and its potential appeal for seekers of all faiths. It is my hope that in sharing this story of Ibn al-Fāriḍ, Francis's contemporary, Franciscans (indeed all Christians) and Muslims will see the reflection of Francis and Ibn al-Fāriḍ in the other, and increasingly view one another as fellow pilgrims on the one *hajj* to the one God.

The present-day mosque and mausoleum of Ibn al-Fāriḍ in Cairo.

ANGELA OF FOLIGNO: POVERTY/*FANA*

PAUL LACHANCE, O.F.M.

Raimon Panikkar, one of the pioneers of current interreligious dialogue, submits that:

> the one who knows only his or her own religious tradition can not truly know it. One must at least know one religion other than one's own in order to properly situate in truth a deep understanding of the one that we profess. That is why I advocate interreligious dialogue so strongly, seeing in it a highly religious act, and not only an intellectual luxury.[1]

I consider it a great honor to have been invited to be part of this ground-breaking forum on Franciscan/Muslim dialogue. I have already learned a great deal from the earlier fertile presentations. It has been my privilege, also, to participate in similar interreligious conversations in the past.[2] And more recently, following especially the lead of Henry Massignon[3] and Thomas Merton,[4] Christian forerunners of Muslim Christian dialogue, I have had the occasion to deepen my awareness of Sufi mysticism. Nonetheless, given the time at my disposal, my contribution can only be a very modest one. It entails a condensation

---

[1] *Entre Dieu et le cosmos, entretiens avec Gwendoline Jarczyk* (Paris: Albin Michel, 1998), 74. Translation is mine. I am grateful to Colette Wisnewski for editing my text and making very helpful suggestions.

[2] Paul Lachance, "L'esperienza suprema di unione con Dio di Angela da Foligno e paralleli con altre tradizioni religiosi" in *L'esperienza mistica della beata Angela da Foligno Il liber: una lectura interreligiosa*, Atti del convegno tenuto in Assisi e Foligno nei giorni 1 e 2 dicembre 2000 (Assisi: Edizione Porziuncola, 2001), 117-49.

[3] Louis Massignon, *Essays on the Origins of Islamic Mysticism*, trans. Benjamin Clark (Notre Dame: Notre Dame University Press, 1998). Also, *The Passion of al-Hallaj Mystic and Martyr of Islam*, trans. Herbert Mason, 3 vols. (Princeton: Princeton University Press, 1982). For an excellent introduction to Massignon, see Dorothy C. Buck, *Dialogues With Saints and Mystics in the Spirit of Louis Massignon* (London, NY: Khaniqahi Nimatullahi Publications, 2002).

[4] *Merton & Sufism, The Untold Story A Complete Compendium*, ed. Rob Baker and Gray Henry (Louisville: Fons Vitae, 1999).

of Angela of Foligno's spiritual journey with a special focus on the summit of her mystical experience where comparisons with Angela's Franciscan poverty and the Sufi understanding of *fana* (annihilation) can be most fecund. Furthermore, I will, on occasion, mirror some of the other parallels I have been able to detect between her experience and the Sufi tradition. But for the most part I will leave that task to my respondent who is much better equipped to reflect more clearly from the center of the mirror, as medieval mirrors would, rather than from the more obscure sightings from the edge.

Over the past twenty years, at least in the English-speaking world, Angela of Foligno has been raised from relative obscurity to rank as an outstanding representative of the Franciscan and Christian mystical tradition. Recently, Bernard McGinn, the premiere scholar on Christian mysticism, in his *The Flowering of Mysticism* – the third volume of his widely acclaimed history of Christian mysticism – crowned Angela as one of the "four female medieval evangelists," the other three being Marguerite Porete, Mechtilde of Magdeburg, and Hadewijch. "Female evangelists" because of the daring and innovative ways in which these mystics described their experiences of God – as one without an intermediary – and the bold claim that, much like the biblical texts, the accounts of these experiences were divinely inspired.[5]

What also seems to strike a chord in contemporary sensitivies is the scorching and completely feminine way in which Angela narrates her dramatic love affair with the "passionate suffering God-man." The intensity of her account, flowing on every page like molten lava, has no match in Christian mystical literature. Thomas Merton, in a conference on Angela, speaks of her ("one of the wild mystics") quite pertinently:

> This is the great truth about her life: In her, passion, instead of being sort of locked up behind doors and left in a closet, becomes completely devoted to God. Passion gets completely

---

[5] Bernard McGinn, *The Flowering of Mysticism. Men and Women in the New Mysticism (1200-1350)* (New York: Crossroad, 1994), 141-42.

caught up in her love for God and in the giving of herself to God.[6]

WHO IS ANGELA OF FOLIGNO?

The main facts about Angela of Foligno are derived from what is referred to as her *Book*. It is divided into three parts. The first part, the *Memorial*, contains the description of the thirty steps that led her into the abyss of the Trinitarian life. The second part, the *Instructions*, highlights Angela's role as a spiritual mother. It contains her teachings in the form of letters, exhortations, summaries of her spirituality and further visionary accounts. The third part, the *Transitus*, provides a brief account of her last moments on earth and a few of her final words. The main focus of my presentation will be on the *Memorial*, the somewhat disjointed account of her journey which she dictated to her confessor, known only as Bro. A. He served as her spiritual director[7] but also transcribed and reorganized what she had told him and, as such, serves as a protagonist of Angela's revelations from God.[8]

---

[6] From a cassette recording (accompanied by Merton's conference notes) graciously made available by the Thomas Merton Legacy trust via Robert E. Daggy, director of the Thomas Merton Studies Center (Bellarmine College, Louisville).

[7] In Sufism the disciple cannot reach illumination without a master. The Sufi mystic Hâfez: "In Love's domain, do not take one step without a guide. For on this road, he who has no guide loses the way," in Javad Nurbakhsh, *The Master and Disciple in Sufism* (Tehran, Iran: KhaniQahi Nimatullahi, 1977), 21.

[8] There has been considerable debate over the "historical" Angela and the contribution of her scribe, Bro. A. The pendulum of scholarship now seems to be swinging towards attesting to the fidelity, even scrupulosity, of Bro. A in reporting what Angela dictated to him even if he was, nonetheless, a filter and organizer of her text. See John Coakley, "Hagiography and Theology in the *Memorial* of Angela of Foligno," in *Women, Men, Spiritual Power/Female Saints & Their Male Collaborators* (New York: Columbia University Press, 2006), 111-30; Jacques Dalarun. "Angèle de Foligno a-t-elle existé?" in *Alla Signoria: Mélanges offerts à Noëlle de la Blanchardière* (Rome: Ecole Française de Rome, 1995), 59-97, and "Perché a te Angela?" in *Angela da Foligno nella ricerca universitaria* (Foligno, 2006) not yet published; Catherine Mooney, "The Authorial Role of Brother A. in the Composition of Angela of Foligno's Revelations," in *Creative Women in Medieval and Early Modern Italy: A Religious and Artistic Renaissance*, ed. E. Ann Matter and John Coakley (Philadelphia: University of Pensylvania Press, 1994), 34-63. Dominic Poirel, "Le 'Liber d'Angèle de Foligno: enquête sur un 'exemplar' disparu," in *Revue d'histoire des textes* 32 (2002): 225-63. Diane V. Tomkinson,

From the scant information about the outer circumstances of Angela's life that can be gleaned from the *Memorial*, we do know that Angela was a married woman, had children and, before her conversion, lived a well-to-do and, likely, conventional life – even if in her eyes a very sinful one. What triggered her conversion, about 1285, is unknown. "Christ's faithful one," as she is called throughout the *Book*, reports, in the first step of the *Memorial* that, at this stage of her life, she feared being "damned to hell" and "wept bitterly."[9] Whatever the cause of her mid-life conversion, it certainly was motivated in part by a dream in which, after she had prayed to St. Francis to obtain a confessor for her, "someone who knew sins well," he appeared to her admonishing her that she should have asked him for help sooner and assuring her of his assistance.[10] The Poverello was to become her spiritual guide and intercessor, appearing to her several times in visions and even, at one point, making the stunning declaration: "You are the only one born of me."[11] The specifically Franciscan identity of Angela is fairly easy to establish. Angela's journey, as I will indicate, clearly bears the markings of the Franciscan way, namely, inner and outer poverty as a path to communion with the disinherited (lepers), union with God, and the consciousness of the interdependency of all created reality. It is conceivable, then, that the powerful archetypal force of Francis's example, so fresh in the memory of the Umbrian populace, was the touchstone that sparked her own beginnings.

Poverty indeed is the dominant theme of her early conversion process as it is described in the first nineteen steps of the *Memorial*, which span a period of about six years. Illumined and set ablaze by the fire and intensity of Christ's love as revealed to her through increasingly vivid and focused visions of his passion and crucifixion, Angela became more and more aware of the shallowness of her past life and the overflow of divine mercy. Gradually, bitter and shameful memories were healed as she grew into the knowledge of self, which becomes one of

---

"The Instructions: by whom, to whom, and why?" Fortieth International Congress on Medieval Studies, May 5-8, 2005, Kalamazoo, MI (unpublished paper).

[9] *Angela of Foligno: The Complete Works*, translated with Introduction by Paul Lachance (New York: Paulist Press, 1993), 124. Hereafter referred to as *Angela*.

[10] Ibid., 124.

[11] Ibid., 277.

the central themes of her spirituality.[12] At this stage of her journey Angela's burgeoning desire is to grow in amorous response to the love she was receiving from Christ by spending long hours in prayer before the crucifix, practicing severe penances, and aligning her life with Christ's, which she later refers to as the "Book of Life."[13] Following the example of her model St. Francis, Angela gradually stripped herself of all her possessions and took steps to become truly poor both inwardly and outwardly in order, as she put it, to become "lighter and go naked to the Cross."[14] In the eighth step, for instance, she confesses that "the perception of the meaning of the cross set me so afire that, standing near the cross, I stripped myself of all my clothing and offered my whole self to him ... the fire of which I spoke drew it out of me, and I could not do otherwise"[15]– an account that is unique in Christian mystical literature. Also, early in her conversion, as mentioned in the ninth step, her mother, husband and sons died of unknown circumstances. Their deaths brought her relief, for they freed her, as she says, to "place her heart within God's heart and God's heart always within mine."[16] Once this poverty has been acquired, it ceases to be an active agent in the development of the story even if the theme will return later not only as a virtue but as an authentic mirror of God and the human condition.

In these early stages (steps seven to seventeen) visions of the Crucified Christ increasingly quickened Angela's journey. Her inner lens

---

[12] Knowledge of self is also an important theme in several Sufi mystics. Anonymous: "Know your own self, if you desire to have knowledge of God: Only he who knows his own self, is one who has knowledge of God." Quoted by M. Fethullah Gulen, *Key Concepts in the Practice of Sufism Emerald Hills of the Heart*, vol. 2, trans. Ali Unal (Somerset, NJ: The Light, 2004), 284. I am indebted to Sumeyye Kocaman for this valuable resource. Ibn 'Arabi: "He who knows himself (or his-self, his soul, his mind) knows his Lord" in *Futûhât al-Makkiyyah*, vol. 3, 308. "He who knows himself knows God" is a traditional saying of the prophet Muhammad.

[13] E.g., *Angela*, 239, 256, 268, 302.

[14] The theme of spiritual nudity, *nudus nudum Christum sequi*, was common at the time. It basically entailed a desire to live in total poverty following the ideal set by Christ, who lived as a poor man and died naked on the cross. Bonaventure developed this theme, especially in his *Apologia Pauperum (Opera omnia)*, vol. 8, 233-320. It was also prominent among the Franciscan Spirituals. For the origins, meaning, and diffusion of this theme, see Réginald Grégoire, "Nudité," *Dictionaire de spiritualité*, vol. 11 (1982), cols. 500-18.

[15] *Angela*, 126.
[16] *Angela*, 126.

became more and more focused as the ties with her newfound lover were intensified. She *looks* at the cross; *stands* at the foot of it to find refuge; *sees* the wounds of Christ "while asleep and awake"; *enters* into the sorrow of Christ's passion suffered by the mother of Christ and St. John; *sees* Christ's heart; *places* her mouth to the wound in his side and *drinks* from the blood freshly flowing from it; *fixes* her attention on the sorrow over Christ's passion suffered by the mother of Christ and St. John in order to experience it herself; and "*encloses* herself within the passion of Christ."[17]

As for her prayer life, Angela said she "found such delight in prayer that she even forgot to eat and her heart was so on fire with the love of God that she never got tired of genuflections or other penitential practices" (step eighteen).[18] For Angela "prayer is indeed where God is to be found."[19] It was part of every stage of her growth. Her prayer life was graced by an astonishing variety of visions, locutions, and raptures. The crucified Christ, the focus of her contemplation, is not a distant reality but increasingly becomes the very dynamic of her life of prayer. As to the forms that Angela's prayer life took she valued repeating, slowly and attentively the "Our Father of the Passion," a devotion widespread among penitents of the time.[20] She also insists that she never abandoned what she refers to as bodily prayer: praying kneeling down, prostrate on the ground, or with hands lifted up toward heaven.

In the seventeenth step, Angela's faith and experience takes a quantum leap. One "different from the one she had before." She also asserts that she had been "led" more decisively into a mystical consciousness of God's inward presence by meditating on the Scriptures and taking "such delight in God's favors" that "she forgot not only the world but even herself."[21] As a result of these momentary but powerful absorptions into the divine life, Angela's psyche was strung to such a high point of tension that she recounts that whenever she heard God mentioned she would shriek, and that seeing paintings of the passion

---

[17] *Angela*, 124-30.
[18] *Angela*, 131.
[19] The remembrance of God is the second pillar of Islam.
[20] *Angela*, 128.
[21] *Angela*, 130.

of Christ made her feverish and sick (step eighteen).[22] The suggestive power of iconography is a constant in Angela's story. The nineteenth step reports that Angela wanted still more from God. God responded that if she indeed gave up her few remaining possessions the Holy Trinity would enter into her.

The twentieth step records Angela's pivotal pilgrimage to Assisi in order, as she puts it, "to feel Christ's presence, receive the grace of observing well the rule of the Third Order of Saint Francis which she had recently promised to accept, and above all become and remain to the end, truly poor."[23] This pilgrimage,[24] a high point of her journey, includes the promise of the indwelling of the Trinity in her soul being fulfilled. Halfway to Assisi, Angela received a numinous experience of God that held her entranced until she reached the basilica of Saint Francis. Once inside, the second time she had entered, she caught sight of the depiction in stained glass of Christ holding Saint Francis closely to himself, a window that still can be seen today. Angela was enthralled, fell into ecstasy and began to roll on the pavement at the entrance to the basilica shrieking, "love still unknown, why? why? why?"[25] – a linguistic phenomena often accompanying ecstatic states and technically known as a *jubilatio*.[26]

It was after this pivotal experience that Angela, having returned to Foligno, began to meet with Bro. A., her confessor. She initially recounted the first twenty steps that we just examined, and mentioned the last ten to him. Then, because of his inability to accurately distinguish one step from another, he condensed and organized the content of these remaining ten of the thirty steps of her journey into seven so-called supplementary steps.

These seven supplementary ones describe the deepening of Angela's perception and mystical ("from within") experience of Christ's passion. The more she penetrated and shared in the suffering of the one she refers to as "the suffering God-Man" and the more she entered into the "poverty" and "contempt" – the triad "poverty, suffering and

---

[22] *Angela*, 131.
[23] *Angela*, 139.
[24] Pilgrimages to Assisi parallel in some way the Muslim pilgrimage to Mecca. Although, certainly not quite as significant.
[25] *Angela*, 142.
[26] For this insight see Giovanni Pozzi, ed., *Angela da Foligno Il libro dell'esperienza*, (Milan: Adelphi Edizioni, 1992), 103.

contempt" summed up her following of Christ – that he had endured, the more the secrets of the divine plan were revealed to her, namely the excessive love hidden in the abysses of the Trinitarian life and manifested by the incarnation and the crucifixion of the Son of God.

In these supplementary steps, Angela's experience of the passion of Christ is not only exterior but becomes more and more interior, "from within" the event itself. For instance, in the fourth supplementary step while gazing at the cross Angela says that she "saw and felt that Christ was within her, embracing her soul with the very arms with which he was crucified."[27] It is also from "within" that she understood not only the sufferings of Christ's body but those of his soul as well. More and more, she affirms that what happened to Christ on the cross no longer saddened her, but rather filled her with an indescribable joy. Witnessing a re-enactment of the Passion on the public square in Foligno, she says, "at the moment when it seemed to me that I should weep.... I was miraculously drawn into a state of such delight that I lost the power of speech, and fell flat on the ground."[28] In a vision which took place on Holy Saturday, Angela entered into the mystery of the Sacred Triduum. Rapt in a rare fusion of the erotic with the mystical she sees herself with Christ in the sepulcher kissing first his breast and then his mouth, from which a delightful fragrance emanated, one impossible to describe. Afterward, she placed her cheek on Christ's own, and he, in turn, placed his hand on her other cheek, pressing her closely to him.[29] Angela, having been married, knew well the gestures of human loving. In this intimate moment in the sepulcher with Christ, Angela experienced its infinite dimensions, a physical expression transformed into the spiritual without the physical being denied.

An incident in the third supplementary step, disconcerting as it is, serves as another indication of how powerfully Angela identified with the path to God traced by St. Francis. In this step she and her companion go to a leprosarium and, shocking as it may seem to our sensitivities, drink from the water in which they had washed the decomposing limbs of a leper. "And the drink was so sweet," both of them reported, "that, all the way home, we tasted its sweetness and it was as if we had

---

[27] *Angela*, 175.
[28] *Angela*, 176.
[29] *Angela*, 182.

received Holy Communion."[30] A similar episode transpired in the life of Francis of Assisi when he drank from the same cup as a leper. As he reports in his *Testament*, encounters with lepers provided the key to his conversion: "when I was in sin, it seemed too bitter for me to see lepers. And the Lord himself led me among them and I showed mercy to them. And when I left them, what had seemed bitter to me was turned into sweetness of soul and body. And afterwards, I delayed a little and left the world."[31] For Francis and subsequently for Angela, lepers were icons of divine revelation. Angela, however, by drinking the very water used to wash a leper, radicalizes Francis's gesture. Repugnant as it may seem to our contemporary sensitivities, the noted French psychoanalyst Julia Kristeva, referring explicitly to both Francis and Angela, observes that "this mystical familiarity with abjection is a fount of infinite jouissance."[32] Catherine of Siena and Catherine of Genoa ate pus from sick bodies. However, Angela's sacramental analogy is unique.

During these supplementary steps a series of stunning Eucharistic visions and experiences – like "a fire of sweet and gentle love" – are also recorded. With these, she is at one with the experience of many mystics, in particular medieval women, for whom visions of the suffering Christ occurred while the Eucharist was being celebrated. In a particularly notable episode which occurred immediately after Angela had received communion, in "an excess of wonder," she reports seeing this world as "pregnant with God."[33] What is even more striking, however, and indicative of the mystical heights which Angela had attained during this period of her mystical ascension, are the formless visions in which she experienced God by way of his attributes of divine perfec-

---

[30] *Angela*, 163.

[31] *Francis of Assisi: Early Documents*, ed. R.J. Armstrong, J.A. Wayne Hellmann, W. Short, vol. 1: *The Saint* (New York: New City Press, 1999), 124.

[32] *Powers of Horror: An Essay on Abjection*, trans. Leon S. Roudiez (New York: Columbia University Press, 1982), 127: "The mystic's familiarity with abjection is a fount of infinite jouissance. One may stress the masochistic economy of the jouissance only if one points out at once that the Christian mystic far from using it to the benefit of a symbolic or institutional power (as happens with dreams, for instance) displaces it indefinitely within a discourse where the subject is reabsorbed (is that a grace?) into communication with the Other and with others. One recalls Francis of Assisi who visited leprosariums ... to give out alms and left only after having kissed each leper on the mouth; who stayed with lepers and bathed their wounds, sponging pus and sores. One might also think of Angela of Foligno."

[33] *Angela*, 170.

tions such as beauty, wisdom, power, humility, justice, and often as the All Good;[34] and by way of symbols such as the "table" and the "sickle." Although not as graphic as the earlier experiences, these contain far more suggestive and enticing power. The ineffable bursts alive in her, combining the transcendental and the personal, a state both sublime and totally inexpressible.

Angela concludes the fifth supplementary step with some reflections on the meaning of Christ's poverty and why, out of obedience to the divine plan, he had chosen it as the highest good. In contrast to the fallen angels and the first parents who claimed being and goodness for themselves as a possession – which is the source of every sin – Christ, in the kenotic movement of his incarnation, passion and death, totally emptied himself and became more poor than any saint or any person had ever been, "so poor that it was as if he had no being."[35] Poverty, for Angela then, is the root and mother of all virtues and is the source of the power through which love is fully emancipated and the soul is established in its complete truth before God. As such it entails the annihilation of the false self, the emptying to the point of nothingness – as demonstrated in the following final steps of Angela's journey – in order to become totally free and filled with the abundance of God's uncreated love and wisdom. Mary and Christ are presented as perfect examples of true poverty.

Angela at this stage of her journey is so certain of the presence of God, her will being united with God's will, that she can declare, in this fifth supplementary step, having attained at once a complete knowledge of herself – her failings, poverty and unworthiness – and a true knowledge of the super-eminent love of God, both together "in a totally indescribable way." Suddenly and inexplicably, however, this spiritual edifice collapses. And it is what takes place in the two final supplementary steps of the *Memorial* which elevates Angela to the ranks of the greatest mystics within the Christian tradition. And it is to these two steps that I will now focus my attention.

---

[34] Parallels could be made here with the ninety names of God which is the cornerstone of Islamic Spirituality.

[35] Pozzi raises the possibility, "given that God transcends being it follows that the union with humanity which is infinitely separated from the divine essence would include an infinite renunciation of his divine essence?" *Il libro dell'esperienza*, 48. Translation is mine.

The Final Steps of the Memorial

It is not possible, within the time available, to do justice to the rich complexity and the dynamics involved in Angela's experience of God in these two final steps of the *Memorial*. It contains some of the highest and most daring expressions of mystical union in the history of Christian mysticism. For our purposes, I intend to highlight those stages which seem to me to hold most promise for a fruitful dialogue with the foundational concepts of *fana* (passing away or annihilation of the I) and its interplay with *baqa* (becoming wholly aware of subsistence, not I) in Sufi mystical experience. These two concepts were personally very illuminating in helping me to understand the co-penetration of the two final steps in Angela's journey. As indicated earlier, for the most part, I leave it in the capable hands of my respondent to further elucidate these concepts.[36]

What is immediately disconcerting about these two final steps is the assertion by the scribe that they took place, almost simultaneously, during a two-year period. According to Bro. A.'s account, the most sublime visions and assurances of the presence of God slightly precede but interlace with the experiences of the greatest suffering and despair – the latter fading but not totally.[37] How these two very different forms of consciousness could co-exist is difficult to understand. Nowhere else in the *Memorial* are we so strongly faced with the dilemma, likely unsolvable, of what part was played by Angela, strictly speaking, in the elaboration of the text and what was due to the influence and reflection of her faithful scribe and confessor.[38] It is clear from numerous affir-

---

[36] See the appendix for my own explorations of these two concepts in Sufi mystics as well as a brief presentation of Rabi'a, who is usually the one referred to in comparisons between Christian and Muslim women mystics

[37] "This sixth step, however, lasted but a short while, that is, about two years. It concurs with the seventh, the most wonderful step of all, which began shortly before it and which follows in my account" (*Angela*, 199).

[38] Lilian Silburn, writing about the mystical experience of "annihilation and nothingness" (which has parallels with Angela's experience), comments in "Le vide, le rien, l'abime," in *Hermes* 6 (1969): 43: "If in the emptying out which makes of the mystic someone ... poor and naked, the unconscious absorptions during which he is reduced to nothing without even knowing it, the annihilation in God and access to Nothingness, are very precise and clearly distinct experiences for the one undergoing them, these do not constitute strictly successive phases. One can be initiated before the end of the preceding one; many progress in parallel fashion and often there are flashes of

mations in both steps that both Angela and Bro. A., in different ways, were struggling to find a language to express the inexpressible and are, in the final analysis, protagonists and co-authors of these astonishing communications from God.

A clue, nonetheless, to a possible hermeneutic for what happens in these final stages of the *Memorial* is provided in *Instruction* 4.[39] An anonymous disciple reports that during an "illumination" that took place possibly four years later during the celebration of the Eucharist, Angela had been drawn and absorbed into the "fathomless abysses of God," and while she was still under the impact of this vision, the crucified God and man appeared to her and bestowed upon her soul, in a perfect manner, "the double state of his own life": the total absorption in the experience of the sweetness of the uncreated God and the cruel death pains of his crucifixion. Commenting further on the nature of the simultaneous reproduction of this double state, the scribe says that while in this illumination, Angela was at once "filled with joy and sorrow, sated with myrrh and honey, quasi-deified and crucified."[40] Similarly, Angela herself, as the scribe reports later on in this *Instruction*, had described a vision concerning her spiritual sons in which: "They seem to be so transformed in God that it is as if I see nothing but God in them, in both his glorified and suffering state, as if God had totally transubstantiated and absorbed them into the unfathomable depths of his life."[41]

We can surmise then – even if there is no reference to them – that the nature of the experience just related in this *Instruction* is akin to Angela's plunge into the agony and identification with Christ crucified, "the horrible darkness" of the sixth step and her immersion into the

---

future realization. This need not surprise us, for in the spiritual experience leading to the atemporal and the undifferentiated, everything is present at every moment. It is very difficult to establish stages as if these evolved in temporal sequence. Moreover, as soon as the mystic lives in Nothingness – dwelling nowhere – empty spaces previously traversed tend to blend with one another so as to become one; in the forgetting of self, in the forgetting of forgetting itself, the mystic constantly loses himself in an abyss about which he knows nothing." Translation is mine.

[39] According to the latest but unpublished study of the manuscript tradition this *Instruction* is a very early one and appears in all the basic manuscripts so that we can be assured of its authenticity. I am grateful to Dominic Poirel of the Institut de Recherche et Histoire des Textes in Paris for this information.

[40] *Angela*, 246.

[41] *Angela*, 249.

fathomless abysses of God of the seventh step of the *Memorial*. The theological implications of such an experience have yet to be fully developed. In the Christian mystical tradition the only comparison that I know of which comes close to Angela's experience, but nowhere near its existential and torturous intonation, is that found in John of the Cross's description of the blessings and the luminosity inherent in the dark night of the soul and of the spirit.

In these two steps, of which more will be said later, Angela seems to be sharing at an unprecedented level and depth the very kenotic movement in which Christ never more manifests divine love than when he climaxes the incarnational process by totally emptying himself of his divinity on the cross and, as Angela strikingly asserted in another context, becomes "poor of himself."[42] Or, in other words, Christ is never more divine than when he is abandoned by the Father and never more human than when he shares the ultimate depths and abjection of the human condition – both modalities taking place simultaneously on the cross. A key Pauline text in the second letter to the Philippians illuminates this moment as follows: "[Christ Jesus], though he was in the form of God, did not regard equality with God something to be grasped. Rather he emptied himself, taking the form of a slave ..." (Phil 2:6-7). To be noticed is that in this text there is no mention of duration nor of transition, neither a before or an after. There are not two events, one phasing the other out but a single breakthrough. The dereliction on the cross is divinized and the humility is glorified not after but in the very act of dereliction and humiliation. The kenotic event then needs to be understood as history seen from within the hidden or uncreated dimension of God and the Trinity and in the irreversible movement in which there are no phases of love but rather one single revelation. As the late theologian Karl Rahner has pointed out in his penetrating reflections on the kenotic passages in St. Paul, in Jesus of Nazareth the self-emptying of God and the self-emptying of the human person coincide. Distance and proximity of God are in some strange way mutually conditioned; emptiness and fullness are one.[43] It is not, Rahner

---

[42] *Angela*, 179.

[43] *Theological Investigations*, vol. 4. trans. Kevin Smith (Baltimore: Helicon Press, 1966), 114. See also, 105-20. Rahner concludes his penetrating reflections of the kenotic passages in Scripture by submitting that this faith phenomenon consists in "the self-emptying, the coming to be, the kenosis and genesis of God himself, who

further submits, that the Son of God became a person through the process of his self-emptying but that fundamentally he is the person and the true God at one and the same time in his dynamic work and activity of self-emptying – a non-dualistic function, one might even suggest of self-emptying or self-negation. Or in still other words, the consubstantiality of the divinity and the humanity in Jesus Christ cannot be properly understood unless as inseparable. To be noted, then, are the assonances between this kenotic emptying movement of Christ as God and man and Angela's sharing, her "inabyssation" or "transubstantiation" in the double state of Christ's life, at once "crucified" and "deified" in the "illumination" just referred to in *Instruction* 4.

Whatever conclusion we may come to regarding the conjunction of these final two steps, it is clear that we have an artificial construct and since it is ultimately impossible to determine precisely how these two seemingly contrary experiences were mingled or to what extent they succeeded one another, for the sake of clarity we are led to follow Bro. A.'s lead and summarize them separately.

The Sixth Step: The Horrible Darkness

As we have already begun to suggest, the sixth step is Angela's version of what was later called and more completely described by John of the Cross as the dark night of the soul.[44] The storm, "the horrible darkness," bearing down on Christ's faithful one had devastating effects on her body but even more on her soul. Concerning the torments of the soul the only comparison that came to her mind to describe her state of desolation was "that of a man hanged by the neck who, with his hands tied behind him and his eyes blindfolded, remains dangling on the gallows and yet lives, with no help, no support, no remedy, swinging in the empty air."[45] In this encounter with total despair in which body and soul tremble in uncontrollable agony, from the lowest depths, the cry of final abandonment rises to Angela's conscious-

---

came to be by becoming another thing, derivative, in the act of constituting it, without having to change in his own proper reality which is the unoriginated origin."

[44] Bernard McGinn in his recent anthology of Christian mysticism selects this sixth step as representative of medieval women's experience of "searing dereliction." *The Essential Writings of Christian Mysticism* (New York: Random House, 2006), 374-78.

[45] *Angela*, 197.

ness. Assuming, significantly, a maternal role, she chooses the words of Christ on the cross as the only ones fitting to articulate her groans of anguish. She wailed and cried out repeatedly: "My son, my son, do not abandon me, my son!"[46] By the power and the very dialectic of Christ's burning love for her, Angela was allowed to enter his final agony and abandonment on the cross. Once again, it is this deep participation in the test of the final hour that provides meaning and illustrates most powerfully Angela's experience of the profound abyss and dereliction. To be sure, it is a partial identification and participation in the passion event. As the theologian Hans Urs von Balthasar points out, "the mystical dark nights, at the most, are distant approximations of the inaccessible mystery of the cross; for if the Son of God is unique, likewise his abandonment by the Father is unique."[47] Angela could do no more than share something of what happened on the cross, participate in some of its inner drama and torment – even if, in transposing Christ's last words as she did, she articulated it in terms of identification unique in the history of mystical literature.

Angela, in this step, is immersed in a dark fire of purification meant to purge the very roots of self-love, unruly passions, and resistance to God's will. Demons afflict her horribly. They not only remove the support of her virtues and revive in her vices with which she was familiar, but also arouse others that had been unknown to her. These rise to the surface with uncontrollable fury. Her body, she reports, is on fire – the residues of sexual disorder – and until she is forbidden to do so, she cauterizes it with the terrible antidote of material fire. Angela is also given a dreadful lucidity about her own sinfulness. She perceives herself as "house of the devil, a worker for and a dupe of demons, their daughter even ... devoid of all rectitude and virtue, and worthy only of the lowest part in hell."[48] She even cries out for death, and beseeches God to send her to hell: "Since you have abandoned me, make an end to it now and completely submerge me."[49] She has fallen so very low that she describes herself "as damned," but adds, "I am in no way preoccupied with this damnation; rather, what concerns me and grieves

---

[46] *Angela*, 198.
[47] Hans Urs Von Balthasar, *Pâques: le Mystère*, trans. R. Givord (Paris: Editions du Cerf, 1981), 76. Translation is mine.
[48] *Angela*, 200.
[49] *Angela*, 198.

me most is having offended my Creator."[50] Finally, it is the last vestige of pride that must be eradicated for it must be completely rooted out if the soul is to be seated in the truth of its relationship before God. For love to be pure, every illusion and every trace of self-satisfaction in any good accomplished must be wiped away. Little wonder that, as the last remnants of resistance and rebellion rise to the surface from their hidden and unconscious sources, Angela, with Job-like utterances, in a state of havoc, rages against the night and her body swells in violent upheaval. The torrent of words and comparisons matches the fury of the assault. It is a battle waged alone in the depths of the soul. There is nobody there to help nor any consolation possible from anyone, not even God himself. The torture is excruciating – a "veritable martyrdom."[51]

Angela needed to live through the crumbling of her most secure foundation in the transcendental life and dwell in a "horrible darkness," a point of no return, a nothingness, in order to find herself, correlatively, solidly entrenched in the depths of God's life as described in the next and final step. The cross of Christ is at the center of this mysterious transformation and reconciliation of opposites. By entering into the mysterious inner world of Christ's passion, sharing even his abandonment on the cross, she experienced a darkness that paradoxically was not eliminated but was integrated and inverted (euphemized) in order to disclose the superabundant light and the inner recesses of the Triune God. Thus instead of a symbol of inexplicable absence, in the next step (or almost simultaneously) darkness becomes a symbol of ineffable presence.

The Seventh Step: The Most Wonderful of All

In the initial vision of this final step the light, the beauty and the fullness that Angela sees in God is so dazzling that it blinds her ordinary capacities of awareness and introduces her to a totally new modality of experiencing God. She says that in this state "I did not see love there. I then lost the love which was mine and was made nonlove,"[52]

---

[50] *Angela*, 200.

[51] *Angela*, 201.

[52] *Angela*, 202. The expression is a collimation with what Eckhart expounds in sermon 83. *Renovamini spiritu* (Ep. 4:23). See *Meister Eckhart: The Essential Sermons, Com-*

that is to say, an experience beyond those described in previous steps on the nature of God's love or her own capacity to love him. Angela's love is being transformed and vested, so to speak, with God's own ineffable mode of loving – which some of the *Instructions* will later refer to as an "uncreated love."[53] This form of "uncreated love" is one which may very well be understood as a negation of the subject-object nature of the relationship, a love of pure relationality – or a love which abolishes the lover and the beloved and perhaps even the loving in order to be pure love: a union with God that is without mediation – a nothingness of both God and self.

To further describe the initial stages of her union with God in this seventh step Angela resorts to the theme of divine darkness drawn from the important revival and development of apophatic mysticism which occurred in the thirteenth century. This current, mostly tied to the Pseudo-Dyonisian corpus and the availability of new translations and commentaries of his work, had widespread success among medieval mystics in their attempt to describe God's unknowability. Using the Dyonisian apophatic language but with a subtlety that is uniquely hers, Angela asserts that she saw God as the "All Good" or the "secret Good" "in and with darkness." "In darkness" to indicate the dimension of subjective blindness or the negative mode of perception and "with darkness" to suggest the transcendental obscurity of the Trinitarian life which she claims she is now perceiving. Angela further asserted that there were degrees of elevation or attraction in these dark visions. In the highest modality, in which she was elevated three times, she

---

mentaries, Treatises and Defense, trans. Edmund Colledge, O.S.A. and Bernard McGinn (New York: Paulist Press, 1981), 208."If you love God as he is God, as he is spirit, as he is person and as he is image – all this must go! 'Then how should I love him?' You should love him as he is a non-God, a nonperson, a nonimage, but as he is a pure unmixed, bright 'one,' separated from all duality; and in that One we should eternally sink down, out of 'something' into 'nothing.'" This non-love of the self finds still another resonance in the same text by Eckhart: "You should love God unspiritually, that is, your soul should be unspiritual and stripped of all spirituality for so long as your soul has a spirit's form it has images, and so long as it has images, it has a medium, and so long as it has a medium, it has not unity or simplicity. Therefore your soul must be unspiritual, free of all spirit and must remain spiritless." I am indebted to Pozzi for this insight, *Il libro dell'esperienza*, 52-53.

[53] For further development of the absolute negativity of the substance of this vision, its non-object and non-subject nature as the "uncreated love" described in some of the *Instructions* (esp. *Instruction* 2, but also *Instructions* 14, 18, 22, 30), see Pozzi, *Il libro dell'esperienza*, 190-92.

says that she found herself standing or lying in the midst of the Trinity and the gravitational pull from the depths of God's Trinitarian life drew her more than anything else: "When I am in that darkness I do not remember anything about anything human, or the God-man, or anything which has a form."[54] Apparently, according to her perception, the most ineffable darkness, symbol of the depths of the Trinity, is one that fades off into one of lesser intensity: the vision of the God-man. In this lesser darkness Angela says that she sees the eyes and the face of the God-man as he graciously and gently leans over to embrace her. And while doing so he tells her "You are I and I am you." It is the moment of mystical marriage so celebrated by the mystics. In this lesser experience of the vision of the God-man, which she says is hers continually, Angela claims that so complete is the union and identity with him that the distinction between object and subject seems lost. She was given the assurance that there was no longer any intermediary between God and herself (*nihil erat medium inter me et ipsum*).[55] In this wedding feast in the night Angela seems to be participating in the very movement in which the Son of God reveals and is in communion with the Father, the inaccessible and unrepresentable dimensions of the Trinity.[56] In this secret Good in which she is enraptured Angela further affirms that she sees nothing which can be imagined or conceived and yet at the same time knows everything she wants to know

---

[54] *Angela*, 205.

[55] *Angela*, 205. A similar mystical experience is described by Bayazid: "My 'I am' is not 'I am,' because I am He, and 'I am' he is He." in *Shatahat*, 111 quoted in Carl W. Ernst, *Words of Ecstasy in Sufism* (Albany: State University of New York Press, 1985), 27; also, the often quoted saying of Ibn 'Arabi (the "Great Master" of Sufism): "He who adores me never ceases to approach me until I love him, and when I love him, I am the hearing by which he hears, the sight by which he sees, the hand by which he grasps, and the foot by which he walks," in Titus Burkhardt, *An Introduction to Sufi Doctrine*, trans. D.M. Matheson (Lahore, Pakistan: Ashaf Press, 1958), 92; the author of *al-Minhaj*: "I do not know whether I am myself or Him. I am in bewilderment, but I am sure I am not myself. I am a lover of the one loved or love itself. I am intoxicated from the cup of Oneness, and I am not myself. What am I? Am I a phoenix with no fame or mark? I am away from my home, and I am not myself. I am transient in soul but permanent by the Beloved. I am flying high, and I am not myself." Quoted by M. Fethullah Gulen, *Key Concepts of Sufism*, 152.

[56] For further reflections on the Trinitarian dimensions of Angela's experience, see Diane V. Tomkinson, "'In the Midst of the Trinity' Angela of Foligno's Trinitarian Theology of Communion," unpublished dissertation, Fordham University, 2004.

and possesses everything she wants to possess. She sees nothing and everything at once.

In this vision of God in the darkness, Angela claims that the body or the soul does not tremble or move as at other times; the soul sees nothing and everything; the body sleeps and speech is cut off – an experience akin to what some of the Greek Fathers described as *apatheia*, a state of tranquility, a perfect control of the irrational parts of the soul which have been reordered to receive the fullness of divine indwelling.[57]

During this period of grace and plenitude Angela is blessed with visions that multiply in kaleidoscopic fashion, ever changing and ever new, often blending into one another. She "swims," to use one of her expressions, in the boundless life of the Trinity, delighting in God's wisdom and judgments.

The dark visions that transmit a heightened awareness of God's transcendence were not, however, Angela's final revelations in this final step of the *Memorial*. There is more. In a subsequent vision, she said that an abyssal attraction drew her ever more deeply into the depths of the Trinity with unction and delights totally beyond any she had ever experienced. In this fathomless abyss all previous supports: the life and humanity of Christ, the cross as bed to rest on, the considerations of the contempt, suffering and poverty experienced by the Son of God (to which she had just alluded), the visions of God in and with darkness, indeed, everything that could be named are as nothing and fade into the background. Angela's use and pursuit of negations to describe the un-nameability of her experience is relentless.

In these supreme experiences Angela distinguishes two modalities through which she experienced God in the innermost recesses of her soul. In the first one, she perceives the manifestation of God in "every creature and in everything that has being, in a devil and a good angel, in heaven and hell, in good deeds and in adultery or homicide, in all things, finally, which exist or have some degree of being, whether

---

[57] For a description of the state of *apatheia*, see step 29 of John Climacus's *The Ladder of Divine Ascent* in *John Climacus: The Ladder of Divine Ascent*, trans. by Colm Luibheid and Norman Russell (New York: Paulist Press, 1982), 282-85. It is likely that this theme infiltrated the Franciscan Spirituals through the influence of the Latin translation of Climacus's work by Angelo of Clareno, one of the leaders of the Franciscan Spirituals.

beautiful or ugly."[58] This modality, one could advance of non-dualistic awareness, is continual. Furthermore, Angela affirms that when she is in this state her soul is given a divine grace "that it cannot commit any offense,"[59] and makes the daring and, at that time, very contested affirmation that she was admitted to a vision of the beatific state.

In the second modality, the manifestation of God is even more direct and the delights exceed, she says, all that can be said or imagined. In this type of presence, intermittent and of diverse duration, Angela received the gift of penetrating the hidden meaning of the Holy Scriptures, how some are saved and others are damned through them. Moreover, in this region of the soul, where she sees the All Good exists, there is a chamber, a place of quietude and rest wherein no joy nor sadness can penetrate.[60] In this state Angela says she sees "the One who is and how he is the being of all creatures,"[61] the supreme mode of essence mysticism. "Alone, purified, and totally celestial," she hears God declaring that in her rests the entire Trinity: "You hold me and I

---

[58] *Angela*, 212.

[59] *Angela*, 213.

[60] Mystics of all ages and traditions have tried to find some term to describe the deepest and most inward part of the soul where God dwells. Gregory of Nyssa called it the "heart," the "conscience," the "minds depths"; Bernard of Clairvaux, a "cubicle"; Bonaventure, "the summit of the mind" or "spark of conscience"; Catherine of Siena, the "interior home of the heart"; Eckhart, "the little castle" or "ground"; John of the Cross, the "substance" or "deepest center of the soul." For a study of this theme see Léonce Reypens, "Ame (structure d'après les mystiques)," in *Dictionnaire de Spiritualité*, vol.1 (1937), cols. 433-67. For several Sufi mystics, in particular al-Hallaj, one of the corresponding terms for this apophatic deep knowledge of God, the secret center of the heart, is referred to as "the virgin point," *le point vierge* in Massignon's parlance. The latter quotes this term in several forms, e.g., in a letter to his friend Mary Kahil, in *L'hospitalité sacré*, ed. by Jacques Keyel (Paris: Le Cerf, 1987), 249. Thomas Merton chose this term to help express what he had experienced on March 18, 1958, on the oft quoted occasion of a new personal awareness which occurred on a crowded street corner in Louisville, Kentucky. Toward the end of his account of this event, in *Conjectures of a Guilty Bystander*, he wrote: "Then it was as if I suddenly saw the secret beauty of their hearts, the depths of their hearts where neither sin nor desire nor self-knowledge can reach, the core of their reality, the person that each one is in God's eyes.... Again that expression, *le point vierge*, (I cannot translate it) comes in here. At the center of our being is a point of nothingness which is untouched by sin and by illusion, a point of pure truth, a point or spark which belongs entirely to God.... This little point ... is the pure glory of God in us.... It is like a pure diamond, blazing with the invisible light of heaven. It is in everybody." Quoted by Sidney H. Griffith, "Merton, Massignon, and the Challenge of Islam," in *Merton & Sufism*, 67.

[61] *Angela*, 215.

hold you."⁶² From this place within, Christ's faithful one understands "the complete truth that is in heaven and in hell, in the entire world, in every place, in all things, in every creature."⁶³ The entire created universe has become transparent to her – a knowledge by communion of the primal harmony of all that is, as seen from within its transcendent source. No part of creation is now strange or alienated. Everything has found its rightful place, "its complete truth."

Soaring from peak to peak in the highest reaches of the human spirit, Angela gives one last example of divine manifestation, one, as she habitually asserts with each new revelation, greater and fuller even than what she had ever before experienced. On the feast of the Purification of Mary, she relates that she was granted to experience her own presentation within the immensity of the divine life. In these ineffable operations, in which she is immersed – "an operation of silence" – Angela says that "the soul cannot understand itself for it is no longer on earth but in heaven." Angela also hears "most high words which cannot be repeated" and the assurance that henceforth "nothing can separate her from God." Once again she makes the bold comparison that this state is "so deep and ineffable an abyss" that this form of presence to God is that "good which the saints enjoy in eternal life."⁶⁴ Throughout this last step of the *Memorial*, Angela has been repeatedly crying out that "words crumble and fall," they "blaspheme," for ultimately "nothing can explain God."⁶⁵

Furthermore, in this supreme moment of inabyssation in God the liminal state that has been implied in the negations that pervade this step become explicit in the unknowing of self which concludes the *Memorial*.⁶⁶ As Giovanni Pozzi comments, "Angela departs leaving an

---

⁶² *Angela*, 215.
⁶³ *Angela*, 215.
⁶⁴ *Angela*, 216-17.
⁶⁵ *Angela*, 213.
⁶⁶ M. Fethullah Gullen in *Key Concepts in the Practice of Sufism*, 248, provides a very helpful description of the fourth and final stage or station of the Sufi's journey and refers to it as "journeying from God." It has remarkable parallels with Angela's experience of God in these final two steps. "This is the state," he continues, "of the special apprentices of the Prophet, which some leading Sufi scholars described as subsistence by God and with God or distinguishing after absorption. Those who have attained this horizon see unity in multiplicity and multiplicity in unity; they experience at the same time two depths with one dimension, and they set out for a new meeting with God at every moment with the pleasure of feeling his company and the pleasure of others

image of herself as one suspended between two abysses, that of the infinite and that of nothingness, that of the unknown God and that of the unknowable self."[67] And as such, her account attains the highest speculative levels of Christian mystical literature.

In the *Instructions*, where Angela's role as a spiritual mother comes to the fore, her sense of the overwhelming mystery of God continues to accompany her until her death. It was only on rare occasions, however, that she agreed to reveal her inner life. "My secrets are mine," she told a friar, one of her disciples, who tried to extricate further revelations from her.[68] In these relatively few episodes of further revelations recorded or in the more didactic texts attempting to describe her higher mystical stages it is significant to note that the language of darkness is never used and there is a growing emphasis on God as "Uncreated Love" (see e.g., *Instructions* 2, 18, 22, 30); the language of speaking of God as "abyss" becomes more frequent and more powerful, as, for instance, in the above mentioned *Instruction* 4 (see also, *Instructions* 19, 32, 35, 36). Finally, in the account of Angela's last days, the *Transitus*, we have a final clue of the total and indescribable immersion in God that she experienced. As she lay on her deathbed, "absorbed more than usual in the abyss of divine infinity" we are told that she cried out repeatedly: "O unknown nothingness! O unknown nothingness!"[69] As in the final stages of the *Memorial*, in the ineffable abyss of her own nothingness, Angela had discovered correlatively the unknowable, unfath-

---

whom they lead toward that meeting. They neither fall into confusion and make utterances of pride that are incompatible with the rules of Shari'a, nor do they show feigned reluctance to attract His mercy. Instead, they always breathe self-possession. They feel breezes of journeying in God in journeying toward Him, and they observe the truth of journeying from God in journeying in Him. They are in a state of having both found Him and lost Him, and of having both met with Him and departed from Him, and of feeling a nearness to and a distance from Him all at the same time."

[67] Pozzi, *Il libro dell'esperienza*, 211. Translation is mine.

[68] *Angela*, 248. According to Gulen, keeping hidden the special gifts they may have received from God is also a characteristic of Sufi mystics: "*Talbis* (Self-Concealment) means that the perfected servants of God who attribute to God whatever good or virtues that they may have, try to be known as ordinary people by constantly keeping secret the special blessings and extraordinary attainments with which the Eternally Generous One favors them, and the blessed times when they come." Cf. *Key Concepts the Practice of Sufism*, 166.

[69] *Angela*, 315.

omable and unnamable depths of the Triune God.[70] The unity in God, one might say, beyond the three persons. The deepest immanence of God in herself coincides with being in the highest transcendence of God's life, both engendering one another in a mysterious co-mixture of identification and distinction.

Angela had indeed experienced the inexpressible and yet tangible love of the suffering God-man that, as she had been told in *Instruction 23*: "his love for her had not been a hoax, but he had loved [her] with a most perfect and visceral love."[71]

---

[70] Thomas Merton, *Merton & Sufism*, 111-12. In his correspondence with Abdul Azizí, his Muslim friend, wrote as follows concerning the most important doctrinal issues dividing Muslims and Christians: "Just as you (and I too) speak with reverence of Allah Rahman and Rahim, so I think you can see that speaking of Father, Son and Holy Spirit does not imply three numerically separate beings. The chief thing that is to be stressed before all else is the transcendent UNITY of God. Now as this unity is beyond all number, it is a unit in which 'one' and 'three' are not numerically different. Just as Allah remains 'one' while being compassionate and merciful, and his compassion and mercy represent Him in different *relations* to the world, so the Father and Son and Holy Spirit are Perfectly One, yet represent different relations.

But there is of course a distinction: Rahman and Rahim are 'attributes' and 'names' of God, but not subsisting *persons*. Here the trouble comes in the definition of person. The idea of 'person' in God is by no means the same as the current and colloquial idea of 'person' among men: where the 'person' is equivalent to the separate individual man in his separateness. This is of course where the confusion comes, in speaking of the 'Three Persons' in God. This naturally conjures up an image of three separate beings, three *individuals*. The idea of Person must not be equated with that of individual. And, once again, 'three' is not to be taken numerically.

The one thing which we must absolutely confess without any hesitation is the supreme transcendent Unity of God, and the fact that there is no other with Him or beside Him. He has no 'helper.' The work of creation and of the salvation of man is entirely His work alone. The manner in which Christianity preaches salvation in and through Christ must not obscure this fact which is basic to the Christian faith, as it is to Islam. The fact is that we believe, as you know, that Christ is not a being outside of God who is His helper. It is God in Christ who does the work of salvation. But here we come to the enormous difficulty of stating in technical terms the Incarnation without making Christ something separate from God, when in fact the humanity of Christ is 'an individual' human nature. This is beyond me for the moment, but I will try to think about it in terms that would be meaningful to you.... There seems to be much in common between our idea of the working of God in and through Christ and your idea of God manifesting Himself to the world in and through the Prophet. I must leave this to future consideration. The one technical difference of a doctrine of the incarnation is of course enormous."

[71] Merton, *Merton & Sufism*, 280.

APPENDIX

From the ninth to the twelfth century, Sufism underwent a remarkable development. In an important essay on the subject of mystical union in Islam, Michael Sells has pointed out that in the path to the Real being articulated by the Sufi mystics one must try to understand two foundational concepts, *fana* and *baqa*.[72] These two concepts are in constant interplay in all but especially in the final stations of the Sufi's search for union with God. *Fana* has to do with the "passing away of the self," and *baqa*, the "remaining of a consciousness that can be to be said to be divine within the human or human within the divine."[73] To pass away or to become empty of self is to become like a polished mirror reflecting the divine image and at the same time to become one with the divine in that image. Interesting examples of this obliteration (*fana*) and returning (*baqa*) of consciousness in the higher stages of Sufi mystical union can be found in the tenth century Sufi Junayd (d.298/910). How ambiguous such a status can be is illustrated by the following quotation by Junayd taken from one of his books *Kitab al-Fana* (Book of Annihilation):

> Then he unveiled over me an overwhelming vision and a clear manifestation. He annihilated me in generating me as he had originally generated me in the state of my annihilation. I cannot designate him because he leaves no sign, and I cannot tell of him because he is the master of all telling. Did he not obliterate my trace with his attribute? Did my knowledge in his nearness not pass away with my obliteration?
>
> He is the originator as he is the one who retrieves.[74]

Junayd's notion of annihilation, even of annihilation of annihilation has interesting parallels in later Sufi mystics such as in Niffari's (d.354/965) discussion of separation and intimate union, the love verses of Rumi (d.672/1230) and especially in the grand master of Sufi

---

[72] "Bewildered Tongue: The Semantics of Mystical Union in Islam," in *Mystical Union and Monotheistic Faith*, ed. Moshe Idel and Bernard McGinn (New York: Macmillan, 1989), 87-124.
[73] *Mystical Union*, 87.
[74] *Mystical Union*, 109.

philosophy Ibn 'Arabi (d. 638/1240). In Ibn 'Arabi's profound teaching on perpetual transformation, union and separation occur simultaneously, the lover perpetually finds and perpetually separates from the Beloved. Similarly for Ibn 'Arabi, in each inhalation the Sufi achieves a new form and in each exhalation gives up the form. The goal for the mystic is to align and fuse his breath with the eternal divine breath as indicated in the following quotation:

> The seeker continues to say with every breath
> 'My lord, increase me in knowledge'
> as long as the sphere of the universe turns in His/his breath
> So that he attempts to make his moment his/His breath.[75]

For further development and illuminating descriptions of the several categories of *fana* (annihilation in God's acts, in God's attributes, in the Divine Being) among Sufi mystics see the chapter on "Fana Fi'llah" in *Key Concepts in the Practice of Sufism*, 145-55.

Thomas Merton was fascinated by the concept of *fana* in Sufi mysticism. For example, the only instance in which he revealed the conduct of his personal life of prayer was in a letter to his Sufi friend, Abdul Aziz who had asked him about it. Merton wrote: "Strictly speaking I have a very simple way of prayer. It is centered entirely on attention to the presence of God and to do His will and His love. That is to say that it is centered on faith by which alone we can know the presence of God. One might say this gives my meditation the character described by the Prophet as 'being before God as if you saw Him.' Yet it does not mean imagining anything or conceiving a precise image of God, for to my mind this would be a kind of idolatry. On the contrary, it is a matter of adoring Him as invisible and infinitely beyond our comprehension, and realizing Him as all. My prayer tends very much toward what you call *fana*. There is in my heart this great thirst to recognize totally the nothingness of all that is not God." Letter to Adbul Aziz, January 2, 1996 in *The Hidden Ground of Love: The Letters of Thomas Merton on Religious and Social Concern*, ed. William H. Shannon (San Francisco: Farrar, Straus and Giroux, 1985), 63-64.

---

[75] *Mystical Union*, 123.

APPENDIX II Rabi'a of Basra

My Islamic friends in Chicago tell me that Angela of Foligno could very well be considered a great Islamic saint and Rabi'a of Basra a great Christian saint. As I will try to develop, very briefly, once again, there are many parallels that one can explore in comparing these two holy women.

Rabi'a al-Adawiyya (d.185/801) is the most famous woman in Sufism, the mystical branch of Islam. In some ways, however, much like with Angela, the available evidence concerning her life is very fragmentary and the historicity of many legends about her are objects of scholarly debate. Though she is referred to, even if very briefly, in accounts of early Sufi saints, the most reliable and complete account of her life and sayings appears as late as, and significantly, in the thirteenth century by the Persian poet Faridu d-Din 'Attar (d. ca. 627/1230). In his *Memorial of the Friends of God*, a compendium of the lives and sayings of seventy-five Sufi masters, Attar, drawing from the oral tradition preceding him, provides a sketch of the life and sayings attributed to Rabi'a.[76]

Attar begins his account by immediately bringing to the forefront the gender issue. How could a woman be included in the ranks of male Sufi masters? His response is to appeal to a number of historical precedents including the important role in the Islamic tradition played by A'isha, wife of the prophet Muhammed and the tradition according to which Maryam, the mother of `Isa (Jesus) will be the first admitted into Paradise at the final resurrection. Attar then argues from the principle that since for God, mystically understood, there are no class or gender distinctions – no room for "man" or "woman"; all are "one and in oneness," – then, as a consequence, from the perspective of those on the path to God there is complete equality of the sexes. In his discussion of gender, Attar also makes two observations – which will not surprise those familiar with Christian medieval woman mystics. One concerns

---

[76] Michael Sells and Paul Losensky provide an introduction and an excellent translation of the section in Attar's *Memorial* which treats of Rabi'a in *Early Islamic Mysticism*, ed. and trans. Michael A. Sells (New York: Paulist Press, 1996), 155-70. For Rabi'a's life and work and her relationship with other women mystics in Islam, see Margaret Smith, *Rabi'a* (Oxford: One World Publications, 1997) and the classic Annemarie Schimmel, *Mystical Dimensions of Islam* (Chapel Hill, NC: The University of North Carolina Press, 1975), 38-40.

the gender reversal entailed "when a woman is a man on the path to God she is no longer a woman" and the other is the widespread stereotype of the "weak woman," as Rabi'a is often referred to, as someone especially chosen to confound and prick the bubble and the pretentiousness of male authority.[77]

The little we know of Rabia's life was that she was likely a slave girl eventually set free by her master. She did not marry and when Hasan of Basra, an early Sufi saint often associated with Rabi'a in anecdotes related to her, asked why not, she responded: "My being is long since bound in matrimony. That is why I say my being is extinguished in me and has revived in him [God]. And since that time I live in his power; indeed I am nothing but he. Whoever would have me for a bride must ask not my consent, but his." When Hassan asked her how she was raised to this level, she said, "By losing in him all that I had found." When he inquired further, "By what method did you come to know him?" she answered, "Oh, Hassan! You know by a certain method, but I know without method."[78]

Rabi'a lived a life of absolute devotion to God. "O my God," she was heard to have said, "my work and my desire, in all this world, is recollection of you and in the afterworld, meeting with you. This is what is mine – you do as you will."[79]

Sincerity and single-mindedness were also hallmarks of Rabi'a's values. In one story, she is portrayed as running down a path with fire in one hand and water in the other. When asked what did this mean, she replied that she will "douse the fires of hell and burn paradise, so that both veils may be lifted from those on the quest and they will become sincere of purpose. God's servants will learn to see him without hope for reward or fear of punishment. As it is now, if you took away hope for reward and fear of punishment, no one would worship or obey."[80]

What is especially interesting about Rabi'a for our purpose is her insistence on mendicancy and absolute poverty in order to achieve union with the beloved. One day an important man came to visit her.

---

[77] *Mystical Dimensions*, 155.

[78] Quoted by Martin Buber in *Ecstatic Confessions*, trans. Esther Cameron (San Francisco: Harper & Row, 1985), 31.

[79] *Early Islamic Mysticism*, 169.

[80] *Early Islamic Mysticism*, 151.

He saw her clothes in tatters. He said, "There are many people who would look after you if you would just give me the word." To this Rabi'a replied, "I am ashamed to ask for things of this world from someone who has them on loan."[81]

As for Rabi'a's intimate relationship with the deity, it found a balance between a sense of awe before the totally other and a disarming casualness in the presence of her Beloved. Her sense of awe before the Most High is dramatically illustrated by a story which tells that once while she was on her way to Mecca, she was left helpless in the desert for several days. She said, "My God, I am sore at heart. Where will I go? I am a clod of earth, and that house is a rock. I must have you." The Real Most High addressed her heart without intermediary: "O Rabi'a, you wash in the blood of eighteen thousand worlds. Don't you see that when Moses – peace be upon him – desired a vision, we cast a few motes of self-manifestation upon the mountain and it shattered into forty pieces!"[82] As for her familiarity which Rabi'a takes with the Deity, it is dramatically illustrated in the story related in which on the way to Mecca during a divine manifestation, she is reported to have said: "You come to me right here!" Rabia took literally that God was indeed her "friend" or "beloved."[83]

Rabi'a's love for God was not only an intimate one but was also devoid of self interest, a central quality of Sufi mysticism. This quality is illustrated by one of her prayers: "O Lord, if I worship you out of fear of hell, burn me in hell. If I worship you in the hope of paradise, forbid it to me. And if I worship you for your own sake, do not deprive me of your eternal beauty."[84]

There are many anecdotes such as I have just quoted which allude to or hint at the heights of mystical union, which Rabi'a had attained, how she was "lost in love-union" and "in her age," as Attar attests, "had no equal in proper behavior or mystical knowledge."[85]

---

[81] *Early Islamic Mysticism*, 167.
[82] *Early Islamic Mysticism*, 157.
[83] *Early Islamic Mysticism*, 154.
[84] *Early Islamic Mysticism*, 169.
[85] *Early Islamic Mysticism*, 155.

Of Veils and Mirrors

Robert Lentz, O.F.M.

My role at this conference is not so much to present an academic paper, as it is to share with you an artist's insights. I am a crafter of images. Visual symbols are my primary language. Through visual symbols I work my way through ideas until I can eventually express my thought in words. I have brought an image to this conference that has startled me from the moment I first conceived it. In its center is a polished metal mirror, related, perhaps, to the mirrors known to our medieval forebearers. Those who have approached the panel and gazed into this mirror have seen themselves gazing back. Above and around the mirror is a fabled Persian bird called the Simorgh. To her right is a hoopoe bird, sitting on a branch, painted not in the style of Middle Eastern miniaturists, but the way a Franciscan artist might paint, aware of the *haecceitas* of John Duns Scotus and the respect our Father Francis showed every living thing. Finally there is a quotation from the Simorgh in Farid ud-Din Attar's *The Conference of the Birds:*

> "I am a mirror set before your eyes,
> And all who come before my splendour see
> Themselves, their own unique reality."

This image is so different from what I usually paint that I have felt myself a stranger in my own studio for many weeks.

The title of this Franciscan Forum is *Mirroring One Another, Reflecting the Divine: The Franciscan-Muslim Journey Into God.* It is a long title with three different elements: our journey into God, the way we reflect God, and the way we reflect one another; and, with the daring of an artist and storyteller, I intend to treat all three in this paper. What I have to say dates back five years to a hot October day in the New Mexican mountains, as I sat on top of a huge granite boulder and first encountered Ibn al-Arabi's thought. It grew during a week of solitude this past February, as I delved deeper into al-Arabi and walked the muddy beaches on Galveston Island. I have held it in prayer for months, even years, and it has crystallized as I have brought one mirror after another into my studio, soon surrounded by round mirrors, trying to find the Simorgh.

As a Byzantine Christian with Russian roots, I am accustomed to veils and the notion of a veiled God. Eastern Christians have always known that the Divine Mysteries are veiled to our eyes, and we have dramatized this awareness with icon screens and curtains that emphasize the limits of our understanding. As a contemplative artist, I know an apophatic God. Traveling in the Middle East, the veil has taken on additional layers of meaning for me as I have encountered millions of Muslim women wearing veils of many types. I believe the veil is an important element in any consideration of a divine mirror, just as I believe, as a Franciscan, that the Christmas creche becomes too easily a bit of sentimental piety when we forget Francis's profound respect for the Eucharist:

> Let everyone be struck with fear, let the whole world tremble, and let the heavens exult when Christ, the Son of the living God, is present on the altar in the hands of a priest! O sublime humility! O humble sublimity! The Lord of the universe, God and the Son of God, so humbles himself that for our salvation He hides Himself under an ordinary piece of bread![1]

So, I add the notion of "veil" as a fourth element in this paper.

As Philotheus Boehner has pointed out, when St. Bonaventure wrote his *Itinerarium Mentis in Deum*, the word *in* in the book's title is significant. He could have used the word *ad*. The goal of the *Itinerarium* was not to lead us up to God, but rather "into God, in the highest affection of love in mystical union."[2] When the planning committee chose the theme of this Forum, they used the same word, but in English, and with the same significance St. Bonaventure intended. The journey we have gathered to discuss is not a trip to Turkey or Egypt. Nor is it simply the path to better understanding between Muslims

---

[1] Francis of Assisi, "A Letter to the Entire Order," in *Francis of Assisi: Early Documents*, Vol. 1, *The Saint*, ed. Regis J. Armstrong, J.A. Wayne Hellmann and William J. Short (New York: New City Press, 1999), 118.

[2] Bonaventure, *Itinerarium Mentis In Deum*, *Works of St. Bonaventure* Vol. 2, trans. Zachary Hayes, Introduction and Commentary by Philotheus Boehner (St. Bonaventure, NY: Franciscan Institute Publications, 2002), 144.

and Christians in political and economic spheres. Our concern is with the esoteric side of Islam and Christianity, and how this side of both religions produces saints who end up mirroring one another. In recognizing such deep similarities we will find a lasting foundation upon which respectful coexistence can flourish. After centuries of mistrust, warfare, and hatred, after the evils of colonization and economic exploitation, in the face of worldwide terrorism, only a foundation anchored in God himself can hope to support what is ours to build.

As Franciscans, we rejoice to be "pilgrims and strangers" in this world. We are pilgrims and strangers after the example of St. Francis, who, in turn, patterned his life on Christ. Pilgrims are by definition people on a journey. Strangers are those who are not at home. Our entire life is a journey into God. St. Clare used the same words, "pilgrim" and "stranger," in her Rule, and gave them even more emphasis when she encouraged St. Agnes of Prague to move "with swift pace, light step, unswerving feet, so that even your steps stir up no dust."[3] Our presence in the Church is a reminder to all Christians that life is, in fact, a pilgrimage.

The Simorgh in my painting comes from one of many allegorical Sufi tales, all of which tales emphasize the pilgrimage character of human life. In 1187, several years after the birth of St. Francis, a Sufi poet named Farid ud-Din Attar completed a long poem called *The Conference of the Birds*, in northeast Persia. He was well versed in theology from childhood, and had traveled throughout the Islamic world. Like many Sufi poets in Persia, he was tried for heresy and banished. Like many Christian mystics in the West, he ran afoul of religious authorities who could not comprehend the subtleties of his mystical theology.

Throughout human history, mystics have struggled with language as they have tried to describe what happens to them in an encounter with the Divine. Language is never adequate. Poetry or song fare better than analytical theology. The experience is simply too big for words. The mystics do their best, only to find religious authorities analyzing their broad paint strokes with a magnifying glass. Experience in prayer is the only validation of what they try to say, and they

---

[3] Clare of Assisi, "The Second Letter to Agnes of Prague," in *Clare of Assisi: Early Documents*, ed. and trans. Regis J. Armstrong, O.F.M. Cap. (Saint Bonaventure, NY: The Franciscan Institute, 1993), 41.

are usually better understood by mystics from other religions than by academic theologians in their own.

Attar's tale is an allegory about the Sufi path. One could say that it is a Persian *Itinerarium Mentis in Deum*. In this tale, the birds of the world gather to seek a king. The hoopoe, a banded bird with a long bill, known for its foul-smelling nest, tells the other birds that they have a king – the Simorgh – but that the journey to reach him is difficult and dangerous. Under the hoopoe's leadership, a large group of birds set out to find the Simorgh. Many fall away, as the journey progresses. Thirty birds eventually reach the mountain where the Simorgh dwells.

Reading Attar's treatise, as he leads a disciple towards spiritual maturity, is so similar to what I have read in Christian manuals that I found myself skimming over many pages. Attar may have been a Muslim theologian from Persia, but the path he described was one I knew from experience as a Byzantine Christian. Once you have traveled the path, reading about it is tedious. You want to skip to the end to compare your experiences with those of others. These paths all lead to a place behind the veil. They are similar because the human condition, with its weaknesses and failings, is the same across the world and down through history. What lies behind the veil is One, spelled with a capital letter. What is behind the Veil leaves one babbling and groping for words.

There is a sense in which the world is a cosmic labyrinth of veils that separate humans from God. Christians speak of original sin. Muslims describe the human condition as forgetfulness. When the great mystic Rabia al-Adawiyya humbly asked God for just one particle of spiritual poverty, she heard God say, "... you are still within seventy veils of self-existence; until you have come forth from beneath those veils, and set forth on the way toward Us, and passed the seventy stations, you will not be fit even to speak of that Poverty."[4] In one of his poems Rumi says,

---

[4] Margaret Smith, quoting Rabia in *Rabi'a: The Life and Work of Rabi'a and other Women Mystics in Islam* (Oxford, UK: One World Publications, 1994), 99.

Have you heard about the king's edict?
He wants all the beauties to come out from their veils.[5]

In the fifteenth century, a wandering love poet named Kaygusuz Abdal said, "For many, what they think they know is a veil preventing them from finding the secret."[6] The great Sufi theologian al-Ghazali taught that the human heart is like a rusted metal mirror that needs to be cleaned and polished before it can reflect the true nature of things. The veil of forgetfulness that covers our inner nature is woven from our passions. It is an interesting fact that Muslim women who are so often veiled in daily life are forbidden to veil themselves while on pilgrimage to Mecca – the Hajj. If things were as they were meant to be, if human beings were not ruled by their passions, neither would womankind, nor the image of God in nature, nor even God's glory be veiled. All of life is about getting past the veil.

When St. Francis and his early followers preached penance in thirteenth-century Europe, what they meant by penance, as Michael Cusato has pointed out, was profound personal and social reform. "To do penance," he writes, "means to begin to consciously distance oneself from and reject all those attitudes, values, behaviors and actions that further fragment the fraternity of creatures, setting oneself over and against another."[7] This is the vision of the Franciscan movement, a vision that places God, rather than the false ego, at the center of the universe. Only with God at the center does the veil over Creation begin to lift so that we recognize our interconnectedness as brothers and sisters, and the value of the tiniest part.

Franciscans talk about the Book of Creation, and how we would not need the written Scriptures if our vision were not so clouded – veiled – that we could not read Creation accurately. Said Nursi, a twentieth century Turkish mystic, suggested that creation is the original form of revelation and that the Koran is merely a commentary on this first "book." Muslims refer to all of Creation as a mirror reflecting the di-

---

[5] Jalaluddin Rumi, quoted by William C. Chittick, "Spirit, Body, and In-Between," in *The Inner Journey*, ed. William C. Chittick (Sandpoint, ID: Morning Light Press, 2007), 164.

[6] Kaygusuz Abdal, *Budalaname*, trans. Sheikh Tosun Bayrak al Jerrahi, in *The Inner Journey*, 172.

[7] Michael F. Cusato, O.F.M., "To Do Penance/*Facere poenitentiam*," in *The Cord*, 57 (2007), 1: 12.

vine Names or Attributes of God. In the *Itinerarium Mentis in Deum*, St. Bonaventure teaches that our mind approaches God through Creation, "... putting the whole world of sense-objects before us as a mirror through which we may pass to God, the highest creative Artist."[8] When seen clearly, in its proper perspective, all of Creation is a mirror of God.

In Islam there is a *hadith* that speaks of a sadness and longing in God: "I was a hidden Treasure and I yearned to be known. Then I created creatures in order to be known by them."[9] According to Ibn al-Arabi, God breathes a sigh of compassion in his sadness, and this sigh, like a cloud, contains all his divine names and attributes in their potentiality. In a similar sense, Franciscans refer to a certain divine poverty – the speaking of his one perfect Word by the Father, a Word that contains all of himself. This Word manifests in Creation the thought of the Father and eventually becomes flesh himself, as the cosmic center. This divine self-giving, so complete that it holds nothing back, leaves God "poor" by the logic of the world. In each instance, whether we speak of the cloud of divine names or the Incarnated Word, we are dealing with a theology of Logos.

If nature is a form of divine revelation and the signs of nature are to be read like signs of a written language, as Said Nursi taught; if all that exists are little words pointing to the one Word, as Franciscans teach: then the point of humankind's pilgrimage is to learn how to read once again. We learn by doing penance, in the original Franciscan sense. When, as al-Ghazali says, the heart has become rusted and opaque so that it is no longer capable of spiritual perception, the rust must be scraped off. "The character of the soul is to love its origin, whom it yearns to meet," according to Sheikh Tosun Bayrak al Jerrahi. "The eye of the heart, which can see the soul, may only be opened by love.... Love is the only force that can rid us of the crust hiding the jewel and weighing us down. Only love can permit our essence to rise to our original state as the best of creation, as the deputy of God, whom he created in the image of his own attributes, to whom he taught all his

---

[8] Bonaventure, *Itinerarium*, 53.

[9] Quoted by Henry Corbin in *Alone With the Alone* (Princeton: Princeton University Press, 1969), 114.

divine names, whom he addresses by saying: "I have created all and everything for you and you for Myself."[10]

When the thirty birds in Farid ud-Din Attar's tale reach the mountain where the Simorgh dwells they are exhausted and broken. They are about to glimpse the Simorgh:

> ... that nameless Glory which the mind
> Acknowledges as ever-undefined,
> Whose solitary flame each moment turns
> A hundred worlds to nothingness and burns
> With a power a hundred thousand times more bright
> Than sun and stars and every natural light.[11]

They are awe-struck and ask how they could ever live in the Simorgh's presence. At the same time they realize that they cannot now live without his presence.

> ... How can a moth flee fire
> When fire contains its ultimate desire?[12]

Love emboldens them and takes away their fear. The Simorgh's herald unlocks the door for them.

> A hundred veils drew back, and there before
> The birds' incredulous, bewildered sight
> Shone the unveiled, the inmost Light of Light.[13]

Once again they are confronted by their sinfulness and unworthiness and they shrink back with shame. The shame and sorrow they feel refines them of the world's weight and they begin to find new life flowing towards them from the brilliant, celestial light they see shining before them. Freed from their sins, they recognize the Light as the source of their own life.

---

[10] Sheikh Tosun Bayrak al Jerrahi, "Travels of the Soul," in *The Inner Journey*, 134.

[11] Farid ud-Din Attar, *The Conference of the Birds*, trans. Afkham Darbandi and Dick Davis (London, UK: Penguin Books, 1984), 215.

[12] *The Conference of the Birds*, 216.

[13] *The Conference of the Birds*, 217.

> There in the Simorgh's radiant face they saw
> Themselves, the Simorgh of the world – with awe
> They gazed, and dared at last to comprehend
> They were the Simorgh and the journey's end.
> They see the Simorgh – at themselves they stare,
> And see a second Simorgh standing there;
> They look at both and see the two are one,
> That this is that, that this, the goal is won.
> They ask (but inwardly: they make no sound)
> The meaning of these mysteries that confound
> Their puzzled ignorance – how is it true
> That 'we' is not distinguished here from 'you'?
> And silently their shining Lord replies:
> 'I am a mirror set before your eyes,
> And all who come before my splendour see
> Themselves, their own unique reality.'[14]

The Persian text contains a powerful pun, for Simorgh simply means "thirty birds."

Roughly fifty years after Attar wrote his long poem, St. Clare of Assisi sent a letter to St. Agnes of Prague in which she penned words almost as astonishing as Attar's: "Place your mind before the mirror of eternity! Place your soul *in the brilliance of glory!* Place your heart *in the figure of the* divine *substance!* And *transform* your entire being *into the image* of the Godhead Itself through contemplation."[15] Several years later she again wrote about the divine mirror "without blemish" to St. Agnes: "Gaze upon that mirror each day, O Queen and Spouse of Jesus Christ, and continually study your face within it, that you may adorn yourself within and without with beautiful robes, covered, as is becoming the daughter and most chaste bride of the Most High King, with the flowers and garments of all the virtues."[16]

The Trinitarian foundation of St. Clare's thought subtly distinguishes her words from those of Farid ud-Din Attar, but each mystic is talking about matters terrifying to any orthodox academic. When I first began work on what became an image of the Simorgh, I consid-

---

[14] *The Conference of the Birds*, 219.
[15] Clare of Assisi, "The Third Letter to Agnes of Prague," in *CA:ED*, 45.
[16] Clare of Assisi, "The Fourth Letter to Agnes of Prague," in *CA:ED*, 50.

ered painting a copy of the San Damiano Crucifix, an icon St. Clare would have seen daily, most of her life, and then setting the mirror over the face and torso of Christ. The result would have been shocking to Christians, at least to those who considered its full implications. Out of deference to Muslim brothers and sisters who would be present at the Forum, I settled on the Simorgh instead. Regardless, the challenge from each mystic to look upon God as upon a mirror and to see oneself is daunting.

Christians know by rote that we are made in the image and likeness of God. Eastern Christians, with their sense of "icon" distinguish image from likeness after Adam's fall by describing our image as distorted. Even so, I doubt most Christians seriously consider what it means to be like God. More shocking are the words of Saint Athanasius, "God became man so that man might become God." When I lecture about icons I often sense ripples of shock run through groups of Western Christians when I point out that deification – *theosis* – is the goal of Christian life. Al-Ghazali and other Muslim theologians talk about "waking up," a process of actualizing the divine image latent in the human substance. Other Muslim theologians talk about "deiformity." This waking up is becoming aware of the Real. It involves all that true Franciscan penance implies. It is to act appropriately by giving all that have rights their right and by accepting one's responsibility before God and creation. It is to see the face of God wherever we turn. These frightening thoughts and many more are contained in the mirror image.

Many Christians and Muslims shuffle through life, obeying moral precepts and observing religious practices, "to save their souls." The exoteric side of religion is as deep as they care to delve. The driving force within both faiths, however, is the esoteric side in which human beings come face-to-face with the *Mysterium tremendum et fascinans* – the Living God, symbolized by the Simorgh in Attar's poem, and he before whom St. Francis cried out that we should tremble and be struck with fear. These living witnesses of the Divine keep our vision of what *we* might become alive. Without them, our religions devolve into moralistic systems unworthy of faith or attention. We end up with a secularized world in which religion is despised as another form of authoritarian control.

The saints – those who have seen – are those who are fully human. Most of us are subhuman, from the traditional Islamic point of view. The norm is the saint, according to Seyyed Hossein Nasr. "... [I]n his being the theomorphic nature of man is chiseled out through spiritual discipline, and therefore he represents the perfect work of art. In the rest of us, that perfection is there, but it's veiled by our human nature. Occasionally it manifests itself, but in the saint the veil is cast aside and the full nature of being human comes out."[17] To paraphrase Henri Corbin, the great al-Arabi scholar, the heart of the saint, in its unveiled state, is like a mirror in which the microcosmic form of the Divine Being is reflected.

Among the many round mirrors I collected in my studio was a circle of uneven pewter that reflected a very distorted image. Only on the last day did I choose the polished mirror over this distorted one. I felt it was important to have a clear reflection looking back at us. For many of us, when we look into the divine mirror, we simply see ourselves with all our imperfections. Seeing God looking back is not some easy New Age gimmick. The birds in Attar's tale were purified by years of wandering and then by successive waves of awareness of their own sinfulness. Ibn al-Arabi points out that when you are looking at yourself in a mirror, it is impossible to see the mirror itself. I found this out the hard way when I tried to paint the name of God on one of my mirrors and kept having to search for the mirror's surface with my brush. As long as we fill the mirror with our empirical self, we cannot see the mirror. We cannot reach the mirror so long as creatures are reflected in it. In the Sufi path, purification is often referred to as polishing the mirror of the heart, so that the eye of the heart can see divine realities previously veiled by the soul's imperfections.

A Franciscan may reply that our Franciscan spirituality does not involve fleeing from the world. Neither does Sufi spirituality involve such flight. Instead it is a question of placing all things in their proper hierarchy of importance, a perfectly fine Franciscan practice, taught by Duns Scotus, the Subtle Doctor. When the good things of Creation are taken out of their proper context, they veil our vision in the divine mirror. When our vision is clear, we see God in all.

---

[17] Seyyed Hossein Nasr, "Echoes of Infinity," in *The Inner Journey*, 66.

At this point it is important to return to the thought of Ibn al-Arabi. The implications of the Simorgh's statement in Attar's poem go much deeper than many Christians might realize. In my week of solitude on the beaches of Galveston this past winter, St. Clare's words about the divine mirror finally began to make sense to me, after years of scratching my head in frustration, only as I delved deeper into Ibn al-Arabi. To go where al-Arabi goes is frightening, for he sidesteps Western ideas about creation *ex nihilo*. If we remember that he is a mystic, speaking from his own very real encounter with the *Mysterium tremendum*, and that he is struggling to explain what is impossible to explain, we may find it possible to stay with his words a bit longer. When we turn to new paradigms from physics, our problems might even disappear.

I must emphasize that my understanding of al-Arabi is that of a novice. I am a Christian and my metaphysics is a Christian metaphysics. Christian concepts such as the nature of the material world are so much a part of my intellectual fabric that I cannot easily leave them behind. For five years I have been fascinated by al-Arabi's thought. Pondering his insights has led me to a deeper understanding of my own spiritual life as a Christian. I want to unfold my response to his insights, as an example of personal growth that comes from trying to listen well to the "other."

While there are ninety-nine recognized Names of God in Islamic piety, al-Arabi and others teach that God's names and attributes are infinite in number. When al-Arabi refers to God's longing to be known, he speaks of a sigh of compassion from God in the form of a cloud that contains the infinite number of divine names and attributes in their potentiality. God creates that he may be known, but his creation is a mirror for himself as well. In creating, he comes to know himself. Each divine name is eternal in its presence in the Cloud, but when it is manifested by God for God, it becomes an epiphany in creation.

Al-Arabi speaks a great deal about the *alam al-mithal*, the intermediate world between the corporeal and the spiritual state, whose organ of perception is the active imagination. Henri Corbin, spends hundreds of pages trying to explain the active imagination, in obscenely long sentences maddening to an English ear. At the root of al-Arabi's thought is the Islamic insistence on the absolute oneness of God, and an attempt, philosophically, not to slip into monism.

Months ago I ran across a theological question in some of my reading that jolted me to the core. If it is in the nature of God to give of himself – to create, to speak his Word, to sigh in longing – has there ever been a time when God has not done so? "Time," here, is of course a contradiction, since there is no time in eternity, no time without the passing of contingent beings. This question emphasized for me once again the absurdity of so much of our philosophical self-confidence. We somehow keep falling into the trap that we can understand the Divine Mystery because of our philosophical systems and our religious dogmas, and yet we always end up, like St. Thomas Aquinas, discovering they are no more than a heap of straw. Mystery remains Mystery.

Connected to this question is the whole concept of creation *ex nihilo*, which has troubled Western philosophers for several thousand years. If God is all that is, complete in himself, and then he suddenly decides to create, one fine day – which sounds a bit like a fairy tale, since there are no days in God's existence *ad intra* – where does matter, as we have understood it in the West for thousands of years, come from? Does God magically produce it from a black top hat? Myth expresses how this can happen in anthropomorphic terms, and all is well. We get into trouble when philosophers and theologians try to dissect myth and prove its logical consistency. The airtight philosophical and theological systems they produce become the criteria religions use to hunt heretics.

I am so much an artist that I often wonder whether I even have a left side in my brain. I mix numbers up constantly, even as I am dialing the phone. I get lost trying to watch sports and end up gazing at moving color. When I try to play chess, I wind up somewhere in my imagination, telling myself chivalrous stories about ideal worlds. Science in general, and physics in particular, baffle me. I am aware of earth-shaking re-evaluations since the time of Einstein that question all our presuppositions about energy and matter. I have tried to understand these discoveries, but to no avail. I have listened to Brian Swimme a number of times, and have fallen under his spell as I have listened, but when he stops speaking, I cannot repeat his thoughts. The new physics speaks of a cosmos that has been expanding from an explosion of pure energy, and of intricate timing in this expansion that has made human life possible. It talks about the quantum vacuum and the strange appearance of elementary particles in this emptiness which simply "foam into existence," to use Swimme's expression, even where there are no atoms, no elementary particles, no protons, and no photons. These particles usually erupt in pairs which quickly interact and annihilate each other. The universe is seething with activity, and it is emerging, not just once, but in every moment. The elementary particles and atoms that make up the universe are not permanently existing objects, but events. The entire cosmos is an ongoing scintillating event. "That which gave birth to the universe is giving birth in this very moment as well."[18]

From what little I understand of al-Arabi's theory of epiphanies, which is the key to understanding most Sufi poetry at its metaphysical core, he is much closer to modern physics than anything in Christian Scholasticism. When al-Arabi teaches that each human being is a unique Name of God, manifested by God to God's Self, it no longer sounds like utter heresy in the light of the new physics. When al-Arabi talks about God's constant creating, he seems once again to be in line with what we are beginning to discover scientifically. When Attar's Simorgh tells the hoopoe and the other birds to look into the mirror that is himself, he is asking much more from them than an inspirational gaze. Here we touch on the *Mysterium tremendum* that lies beneath our tamed notions of having been created in God's image and likeness. God says, "Look at me and you will see yourself." How true this is, once we have cleansed our hearts from all the rust and the scum.

I mentioned earlier how al-Arabi finally unlocked St. Clare's ideas about the divine mirror for me. I still may not understand St. Clare the way a scholar might, just as I may have misunderstood al-Arabi. All I know is that as I walked in silence along the Gulf Coast, under leaden February skies, what al-Arabi said about the infinite number of God's Names connected with my Catholic belief in the Mystical Body of Christ and St. Clare's divine Mirror. Christ is the cloud of divine Names that al-Arabi spoke about. As the perfect and only Word of the Father, he contains every divine Name. His paschal mystery births what we call by the Germanic word "Church," which is the making up of his fullness by the members of his Mystical Body. When St. Clare tells St. Agnes to gaze on Christ the Mirror, she is telling her to find that name of Christ which she, and only she, is. She is telling her to gaze upon what God has intended from all eternity to reveal about

---

[18] Brian Swimme, *The Hidden Heart of the Universe* (Maryknoll: Orbis Books, 2000), 104. This entire paragraph is heavily indebted to Swimme, 90-104.

himself in her. She is challenging her to manifest clearly this unique face of Christ to the world, this face which contributes essentially to the fullness of the Mystical Body. She is talking about St. Agnes as Christ: "Place your heart *in the figure of the* divine *substance!* And *transform* your entire being *into the image* of the Godhead Itself through contemplation."[19]

Having written these things, I am confounded by my own reality and how far I am from this ideal. I am a bedraggled bird miles from the Simorgh's mountain throne. I have glimpsed the mountain from time to time, and have seen from a distance the light that rises from it. These glimpses encourage me to continue as a pilgrim and stranger, hopefully more swiftly now so that my steps stir up less dust. The example of the saints of Christianity and Islam spur me forward.

In her Testament, St. Clare speaks clearly of the mirror we are to be to one another:

> With what eagerness and fervor of mind and body, therefore, must we keep the commandments of our God and Father, so that, with the help of the Lord, we may return to Him and increase of His *talent* (cf. Matt 25:15-23)! For the Lord Himself has placed us not only as a form for others in being an example and mirror, but even for our sisters whom the Lord has called to our way of life as well, that they may in turn be a mirror and example to those living in the world. Since the Lord has called us to such great things that those who are to be a mirror and example to others may be reflected in us, we are greatly bound to bless and praise God and be all the more strengthened to do good in the Lord.[20]

When I was in Istanbul two months ago, my companions and I had dinner at the home of devout Muslims one night. Standing outside before we returned to our hotel, I complimented our host on the beauty of his home. Because he thought I was referring to his furniture, I told him that the beauty I saw there came from his heart and the hearts of his family members. He told me, "A believer is a mirror of a believer." Almost a week later, I mentioned this comment to other Muslim

---

[19] Clare of Assisi, "The Third Letter to Agnes of Prague," in *CA:ED*, 45.
[20] Clare of Assisi, "The Testament (1247-1253)," in *CA:ED*, 57.

friends in the city and a theological student told me the expression was one of the *hadiths* of the Prophet. I asked him for the Arabic, and another friend promised me not only the Arabic, but the Arabic in beautiful calligraphy. The result hangs here in a frame beneath the image of the Simorgh and her mirror.

This story takes on an additional layer of meaning when I tell you that the friend who gave me the framed calligraphy had asked for a Franciscan cord, like the one we wear on our habits, when I visited his house two years before. We had spoken that night about the Franciscan movement and its similarities to the Gulen Movement in modern Turkey, as well as its possible connections with Sufism many centuries ago. We had talked about prayer and the love of God. His request for a cord surprised me, but he may have been just as surprised to see a medallion with the ninety-nine Names of God attached to my habit rosary. I sent him the cord he requested after I returned to the United States. The calligrapher he hired to write the hadith created a mirror within the Arabic letters, so that the two words "believer" look back at each other. This friend has mirrored for me what it is to be in love with God, and perhaps I have done the same for him.

Just before Christmas last year, I had another dramatic experience of divine mirroring, in Konya, a city in central Turkey. It was rather late in the evening, after a long, cold, windy day. Fatih called my room, just as I was climbing into bed, and asked me to come down to the hotel lobby. I found him there, sitting next to a burly policeman I had never seen before. The policeman had come across an old Greek Orthodox liturgical book in the ruins of an abandoned church a number of years ago. Suspecting that it had cultural value, he had taken it to the ministry of antiquities. Curators confirmed that the book was several hundred years old. As they leafed through it, they found a small paper icon from the nineteenth century that was damaging the older pages of the book. When they threw it away, the policeman rescued it from the wastebasket. He later wrapped it carefully in clear cellophane and carried it for years, hoping to find a way to place it in the right hands. At that point of his story, he removed the packet from a pocket in his jacket and handed it to me.

The paper icon was brown with age. It depicted the baptism of Christ in the Jordan River. I was speechless. In and of itself, it had little value. Artistically, it was hideous. Although it may have dated from the nineteenth century, it was not old enough to be a true antique. It was simply a cheap print that a pious priest or deacon had stuck in the book one day to mark his place. On a completely different level, however, this brown piece of paper, so carefully protected by cellophane, had now become a window into the soul of a policeman I would never have noticed in other circumstances. He, a Muslim whose faith forbade the use of religious icons, had rescued an icon for Christians he had not yet met, because of his respect for their beliefs. I hold here in my hand the icon he gave me, a mirror, a glimpse of a soul very close to God.

While these are dramatic examples of encountering divine mirrors in my life, they are not isolated experiences. Muslim brothers and sisters have reflected God's face to me for many years. The centuries of animosity between Muslim and Christian believers in our two faiths must come to an end. As the *hadith* reminds us, we are mirrors to one another. If we will clean the rust and scum from our hearts we will see this very clearly. With our hearts thus cleansed we will recognize the Divine Names each one of us manifests to the world and to God himself.

Originally the image of the Simorgh and mirror was meant to be the centerpiece of a triptych. I envisioned two side panels with matching decorative frames holding a Franciscan and a Muslim saint. These two saints would be examples of mystics whose lives had reflected one another. For many reasons, the triptych never materialized. Perhaps it is just as well, since every few weeks I would find two or three new saints who would vie for a place in the triptych, until I finally realized it would take nothing less than a book even to make a beginning. Our saints resemble one another so much that they might be mistaken for one another at first glance. This should not be surprising since a saint is nothing less than a clear reflection of God and there is only one God.

As I tried to focus on this paper and its theme, I had the same difficulty I was having in choosing paired saints. How easily I might have written half a dozen other papers. As much as I enjoyed comparing St. Clare with Attar and al-Arabi, I might as easily have juxtaposed al-Arabi with Duns Scotus and his teaching about *haecceitas*. I might have written a fascinating paper comparing Clare with Rabia al-Adawiyya, and how each embraced poverty in her pursuit of the divine Beloved. Blessed Jacopone da Todi often sounds like Rumi and other Sufi saints when he talks about holy foolishness, and there are many stories in the life of Said Nursi in which he shows a love for animals that mirrors that of Francis and his followers. How easily I might have compared the early years of the Franciscan movement with the rise of the contemporary Gulen movement in Turkey. I hope some day to compare the Franciscan movement with Sufi brotherhoods in general. And this list could go on and on.

This is the second Franciscan Forum that has taken on the theme of Muslim-Franciscan dialogue. Muslims are beginning to discover Franciscans and Franciscans are falling in love with Muslims. We mirror one another in so many ways that continued dialogue seems a divine imperative. We Franciscans have a sainted father who once crossed the known world to embrace a Muslim sultan. We are called to be peacemakers. We preach a penance that fosters universal fraternity. Where do we go from here, brothers and sisters? How do we keep this dialogue alive and growing?